MAR 3 0 2003

6/22/03 ①

D0852430

LAS VEGAS-CLARK COUNTY
LIBRARY DISTRICT
833 LAS VEGAS BLVD, N
LAS VEGAS, NEVADA 89101

DISCARD

hosting WEDDING *parties*

Unique Showers & Celebrations for Toasting the Bride & Groom

Copyright © 2001
Creative Publishing international, Inc.
5900 Green Oak Drive
Minnetonka, Minnesota 55343
1-800-328-3895
All rights reserved
Printed in U.S.A.
www.howtobookstore.com

President/CEO: David D. Murphy

HOSTING WEDDING PARTIES
Created by: The Editors of Creative Publishing international

Executive Editor: Elaine Perry
Senior Editor: Linda Neubauer
Project Manager: Kathi Holmes
Senior Art Director: Stephanie Michaud
Art Director: Mark Jacobson
Desktop Publishing Specialist: Laurie Kristensen
Food Editor: Ellen Boeke
Editorial Intern: Andrew Karre
Project & Prop Stylist: Joanne Wawra
Samplemakers: Karen Cermack, Arlene Dohrman
Photo Stylists: Jennifer Bailey, Arlene Dohrman, Joanne Wawra
Food Stylists: Ronald Johnson, Abigail Wyckoff
Studio Services Manager: Marcia Chambers
Director of Photography: Charles Nields
Photographers: Tate Carlson, Andrea Rugg
Director of Production Services: Kim Gerber
Contributors: C.M. Offray and Son, Inc.; Fountain Builder;
  Great Entertaining.com

Special thanks to the following for the use of their homes:
  Carol & Jim Bracke; Arlene & Jerry Dohrman; Tony Eiden
  of Tony Eiden Company; Howard H. Johnson of The
  Christopher Inn; Connie McQuire of Centex Homes

Library of Congress Cataloging-in-Publication Data

Hosting wedding parties : unique showers & celebrations for toasting the
bride & groom.
    p. cm.
  Includes index.
  ISBN 0-86573-436-4 (pbk.)
  1. Weddings--United States--Planning. 2. Showers (Parties)--United
States--Planning.   I. Creative Publishing International.
  HQ745 .H67 2001
  395.2'2--dc21
            2001017258

ISBN 0-86573-436-4

Printed on American paper by:
R. R. Donnelley & Sons Co.
10 9 8 7 6 5 4 3 2 1

Creative Publishing international, Inc. offers a variety of
how-to books. For information write:
    Creative Publishing international, Inc.
      Subscriber Books
    5900 Green Oak Drive
    Minnetonka, MN 55343

Due to differing conditions, materials, and skill levels, the
publisher and various manufacturers disclaim any liability for
unsatisfactory results or injury due to improper use of tools,
materials, or information in this publication.

All rights reserved. No part of this work covered by
the copyrights hereon may be reproduced or used in
any form or by any means—graphic, electronic, or
mechanical, including photocopying, recording, taping
of information on storage and retrieval systems—without the
written permission of the publisher.

hosting WEDDING parties

Unique Showers & Celebrations for Toasting the Bride & Groom

CREATIVE PUBLISHING international

MINNETONKA, MINNESOTA

www.howtobookstore.com

c o n t e n t s

A wedding is perhaps the most celebrated occasion in a person's life, made even more memorable by the parties, showers, and receptions that lead up to and follow it. Wedding party hosts, those generous souls who open their homes, their hearts, and their wallets, enrich the wedding experience for their dear friends or relatives. *Hosting Wedding Parties* is designed to help anyone host a successful party that will be fondly remembered by the bride and groom and all of their guests.

The wedding shower originated from the medieval expectation that a bride must enter a marriage with a sizable dowry. A young Dutch girl had fallen in love with a miller who, because of his benevolent heart, had given most of his possessions to the poor. Her father refused them his blessing and his wealth, leaving the daughter without a dowry and, consequently, unable to marry. Out of gratitude for the miller's lifelong charity, the community banded together and "showered" the girl with gifts to fill out her dowry. The couple married and lived happily ever after.

Traditionally, the wedding shower has been an event for the bride and her female friends and relatives. Gifts of kitchenware and bed, bath, and table linens have been showered on the bride because, after all, she would be the one who used and cared for these items in the marriage. The bride and her parents did most of the wedding planning and preparation—the groom just had to make sure he showed up at the ceremony on time.

Today's groom is more active in planning and preparing for the wedding. The conventional gender roles of breadwinner and homemaker have been properly left in the past, so it makes sense that wedding showers are now often planned for both the bride and groom. This opens up a new realm of possibilities for party themes. Shared interests of the bride and groom—golfing, gardening, cooking, or mountain climbing—can become the focal point for a gift-giving party.

Some traditions continue to thrive, such as the engagement party, hosted by parents or close friends of the newly betrothed couple. Congratulatory wishes, reminiscences of childhood, and toasts to the happy twosome all combine to spark their journey to the altar. The bridesmaids' tea, a delightful variation of this girls-only get-together, celebrates the special bond between the bride and her attendants. The rehearsal dinner, customarily hosted by the groom's family, can have a fanciful theme and flavor, setting it apart from the wedding as a time for members of the wedding party to relax and feel appreciated.

The wedding experience is unique for every couple, and these parties can be easily tailored to fit the personalities and wishes of the honored guests. A couple may marry privately, for instance, or at a location too far away for guests to conveniently travel. A delayed party, like the luau reception, provides an opportunity for friends and relatives to rejoice with the newlyweds in a fun-filled, easygoing atmosphere. The same party plans could be used to host a fabulous engagement party or trimmed down in size to become a pool party shower. The garden shower can be easily transformed into an après-golf outing, with recipes

used to supplement a backyard barbecue. Or the bridesmaids' tea party might be adapted to suit a sorority sisters' shower.

Although hosting a party can be taxing and time-consuming, careful planning and advance preparation make the task much more enjoyable. To make the job even easier, six unique wedding parties have been organized here for you. Invitations, decorations, party favors, table settings, menus, and recipes are all completely planned out and ready to put into action. A section of helpful entertaining basics has been added to take the guesswork out of perfect party hosting. Lavish photographs provide inspiration, and step-by-step instructions show you how to make it happen.

These plans are a great jumping-off point from which even a novice host can leap to the party-hosting hall of fame. Armed with detailed schedules and lists and this hefty support team of ideas and expertise, you, too, can host the perfect wedding party.

parties

engagement party

*j*ewel-tone colors and sparkling metallic accents set the scene

for this semiformal party to congratulate the newly engaged

couple. Candlelight glinting off shaped wires and bright glass

beads reflects the spark of excitement in the air. Traditionally

given by the parents or very close friends, the celebration toasts

the future bride and groom and brings together their separate

circles of family and friends. ◆

Fancy appetizers and desserts, set up on separate buffets, give guests plenty of opportunity to mingle and become acquainted. Finger-food delicacies can be set out early and nibbled at leisure, allowing the party hosts as well as the guests of honor to join in the partying. A formal announcement of the engagement is followed by toasts and applause as the hosts and guests show their admiration and support for the newly betrothed. ◆

Keepsake invitations

feature the betrothed couple's engagement photograph mounted in metallic paper. The card transforms easily into a standing frame, a visual reminder as the party date draws near. ◆

MATERIALS

- Blank single-fold cards, 6¾" × 5" (17 × 12.5 cm) with envelopes
- Cover-weight paper in matching color to make stands
- White cover-weight paper for cover announcement
- Metallic paper
- Corner slot punch
- Engagement photo, 4" × 6" (10 × 15 cm)
- White vellum for inner message
- Paper-backed double-stick tape

1 Print card announcement on white cover-weight paper; cut. Cut frame from metallic paper, scant ⅜" (1 cm) larger than announcement. Punch the frame corners with corner slot punch. Mount announcement in frame; secure to card front.

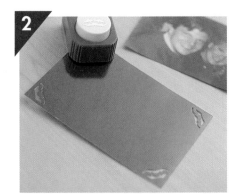

2 Cut metallic paper frame scant ⅜" (1 cm) larger than photo. Punch frame corners with corner slot punch. Mount photo in frame; secure to lower inside half of card.

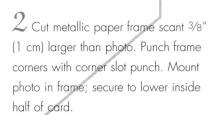

3 Print the party invitation message on sheer vellum paper; include simple instructions for converting the invitation to a standing frame. Cut message to same size as photo; insert corners into slots over photo.

4 Transfer easel pattern to cover-weight paper; cut out as many easels as needed. Glue to top inside center of card, aligning bottom edge of easel support to top edge of card. Apply double-stick tape strips to lower back corners of card. DO NOT REMOVE PROTECTIVE PAPER BACKING.

Elegant nametags identify the guests by name and by their relationship to the bride or groom. Guests can choose to either pin on their tags or secure them with magnets, protecting delicate fabrics. Inscriptions are worked out on the computer and printed on card stock. Individual tags are then cut into rectangles and applied to metallic card stock rectangles, using the corner slot punch that was used to make invitations. ◆

HINT

Nametags should be attached just below the guest's right shoulder. Upon being introduced, when two people shake hands, their eyes easily travel up the right arm to the nametag, helping them commit to memory the name and relationship of the person they have just met.

Reminiscence and

anticipation combine in a photo display of the future bride and groom that records their individual life paths up to their meeting and courtship. Continuing the party theme, photos are mounted in metallic papers and held in coiled wires above jewel-tone glass bottles. Glass beads adorn the top of engagement photo frame. ◆

MATERIALS

- *Photos of the bride and groom from birth to adulthood; engagement photo*
- *Decorative paper for mounting photos*
- *Decorative corner slot punch (same as for invitation)*
- *Craft wires of various gauges and colors; wire cutter; round-nose pliers*
- *Small jewel-tone glass bottles with cork stoppers, or clear cork-stopped bottles filled with water that is colored with jewel-tone food dyes (inset)*
- *Jewelry head pins; assorted glass beads; jewelry glue*
- *Plain wooden frame for engagement photo; jewel-tone metallic paint*
- *Drill and 1/16" drill bit*
- *Silk table runner (page 22)*
- *Coiled, beaded wire, as for floating candle inserts (page 23)*

1 Cut rectangles of metallic papers, ⅜" (1 cm) larger than photos. Punch corner slots; insert photos.

2 Cut wire 8" to 12" (20.5 to 30.5 cm) long. Make a flat coil at one end for holding photo. Curve and bend remaining wire as desired. Insert into bottle cork; insert photo into coil. Repeat for each photo stand, using assorted wires.

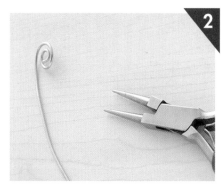

3 Paint frame. Drill holes into frame top, spaced ½" to 1" (1.3 to 2.5 cm) apart. Slide two or three beads onto head pin; cut pin ¼" (6 mm) beyond lower bead. Apply glue to hole; insert head pin. Repeat across frame top. Insert photo.

4 Place a box or other object suitable for a riser in the center of the display surface. Cover with silk table runner (page 22); scrunch and flip runner, as desired.

5 Place engagement photo on riser. Arrange bottle photo stands on each side of framed engagement photo, with bride-to-be on one side and groom-to-be on the other. Expand beaded wire coil (page 23) and arrange among bottles.

In tribute to the betrothed, champagne is poured and glasses are raised. Adding a special touch, glass stems are bejeweled with coiled wire and glass beads, each individualized with a charm. ◆

MATERIALS

- Craft wires in various colors
- Wire cutter
- Multicolored glass beads
- Chain-nose jewelry pliers
- Charms
- Jump rings
- Champagne glasses

1 Cut wire into 9" (23 cm) pieces. Slip a colored bead onto one end. Using chain-nose pliers, make small loop in wire end to secure bead.

2 Attach charm to jump ring; slip onto wire. Attach another colored bead to other end of wire, as in step 1.

3 Twist wire tightly around champagne glass stem, so that charm hangs near center.

A dazzling cobalt blue champagne bucket is emblazoned with the groom's monogram. While permanent etching is a fairly easy procedure, any mistakes cannot be corrected. Faux etching, using specialty paint that dries to a durable finish, produces similar results with far less risk. ◆

MATERIALS

- Glass champagne bucket
- Glass surface conditioner
- Adhesive-backed monogram stencil, such as Monogram Magic™ by Delta
- Masking tape
- White translucent glass paint
- Cosmetic sponge

1 Apply surface conditioner to glass surface. Allow to dry for at least 15 minutes, but no more than 4 hours. Press stencil firmly onto glass; smooth out any air bubbles. Mask off surrounding glass area as necessary.

2 Apply white paint, using cosmetic sponge; use an up-and-down pouncing motion. Remove the stencil before the paint dries. Allow the paint to dry at least 20 minutes before touching.

3 Follow paint manufacturer's directions for curing. To clean, wash gently by hand only; do not soak.

A white napkin wrapped around the neck of the champagne bottle to catch drips is also monogrammed with the groom's initial. The monogram can be stitched by machine or stenciled with fabric paint. Or a purchased monogram can be fused in one corner. ◆

Sheer jewel-tone ribbons are easily transformed into snazzy candy pouches for the guests.

Cinched closed with twisted, jeweled wires, they rest in a luxurious velveteen-padded box. ◆

MATERIALS

- *Shallow, cardboard, heart-shaped box in desired size*
- *Metallic paint in desired jewel-tone color*
- *Gold leaf sizing*
- *Sea sponge*
- *Metallic leaf flakes or foil*
- *Thin cardboard*
- *Batting*
- *Velveteen in desired jewel-tone color*
- *Craft glue*
- *Wide sheer ribbons in jewel-tone colors*
- *Sewing machine; thread*
- *Wrapped candy*
- *Craft wires; wire cutter*
- *Multicolored glass beads*

1 Paint the entire box, inside and out. Allow to dry. Apply leaf sizing in dappled pattern to box top, using sea sponge. Allow to set, following manufacturer's directions. Apply metallic leaf; brush away excess.

2 Cut a cardboard heart shape slightly smaller that the inside box bottom; repeat for the batting. Cut a velveteen heart shape 1" (2.5 cm) larger than the box bottom. Glue batting to cardboard. Center velveteen heart over batting; place fabric side down on work surface. Clip outer edge of design every ½" (1.3 cm) up to cardboard. Apply diluted craft glue to cardboard edge; wrap clipped fabric edge over cardboard edge to secure. Insert padded heart into box bottom.

3 Cut ribbon strips 12" (30.5 cm) long. Fold under 1½" (3.8 cm) on each end; then fold in half. Beginning 1" (2.5 cm) from folded ends, stitch sides together, using narrow zigzag stitch, forming small pouch.

4 Fill pouch with foil-wrapped candy. Twist top closed; secure with wire. Slide beads onto wire; coil wire ends.

Lustrous dupioni silk table runners liven the party with their bright colors. Beaded ends hang luxuriously over the table edge. Easy to sew, these runners can be made in any size to suit your tables. ◆

MATERIALS

- *Dupioni silk or other lustrous fabric in desired colors*
- *Sewing machine, thread*
- *Fusible web strip*
- *Large colored glass beads*
- *Seed beads*
- *Beading needle and beading thread*

1 Cut two strips of fabric, each 1" (2.5 cm) longer and wider than the desired finished length and width of the runner. Two different colors may be used for each runner, as the runner will be reversible. Pin the fabrics, right sides together, matching the outer edges. Stitch ½" (1.3 cm) seam all around, leaving an opening on one side.

2 Press the seam allowances open. Turn the runner right side out. Fuse the opening closed, using a strip of fusible web.

3 Hand-stitch beads along the runner ends, as shown in the diagram. Secure each bead set with an extra stitch in the fabric.

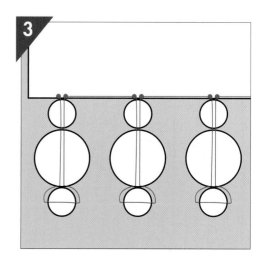

Spirals of wire dotted with colorful glass beads are magnified under water in glass cylinders. The light from floating candles bounces off metal serving pieces and amplifies the glimmering shots of color. ◆

MATERIALS

- *Wire in a variety of gauges (16- to 22-gauge) and colors (copper, gold, aluminum). Do not use galvanized steel. Two wires must be small enough to insert through beads.*
- *Cylindrical object smaller than inside of glass cylinder*
- *Glass cylinder vases*
- *Colored glass or acrylic beads*
- *Wire cutter*
- *Distilled water*
- *Floating candles*

1 Wrap heaviest wire around a cylindrical object, forming a coil; remove coil. Loosen and widen coil as necessary to fit inside glass cylinder to about two-thirds its height.

2 Slip several beads onto finer wire. Wrap tightly several times at one end of coil, enclosing both ends. Wrap loosely around base coil, securing beads in various locations. Secure at opposite end. Repeat with second thin wire.

3 Insert wrapped coil in glass cylinder. Just before party, fill with distilled water to at least 1" (2.5 cm) above coil. Carefully place floating candle on top of water.

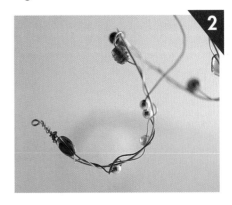

Up to 1 week ahead:
- Make crusts for tarts.
- Make grocery list.

2 or 3 days ahead:
- Get groceries, except shrimp.

1 day ahead:
- Make cheese squares; chill.
- Make Gingered Shrimp and Crab Spread and the Spinach Spread for crostini.
- Finish tarts.
- Make filling and chili sauce for tortillas; combine, simmer, and chill filling.
- Make custard for tortes.

Morning of:
- Assemble tortes; chill.
- Purchase shrimp and prepare according to recipe (could be done a day ahead, if desired).
- Make Blue Cheese-Pecan Spread for crostini.
- Toast crostini bread slices.

4 hours before:
- Assemble tortillas.

2 hours before:
- Cut cheese squares and arrange on baking sheets.
- Slice tortes; garnish and chill.

1 hour before:
- Set out shrimp, crostini spreads and toasts, and tarts.

Just before serving:
- Set out tortillas and tortes.
- Heat cheese squares.

Goat Cheese Squares

2 cups large-curd cottage cheese

6 eggs

1 clove garlic, crushed

1 1/2 cups all-purpose flour

1 cup milk

10 oz. goat cheese (chèvre)

2 cups shredded Monterey Jack cheese

6 tablespoons melted butter, divided

1 teaspoon dried thyme leaves

1/4 teaspoon cayenne pepper

1 1/3 cups homemade bread crumbs*

Makes about 100 squares

Heat oven to 350°F. Spray a 10" × 15" sheet pan with nonstick vegetable cooking spray.

In food processor, combine cottage cheese, eggs, and garlic. Process until smooth. Add flour and milk; process until smooth. Add goat cheese, Jack cheese, 4 tablespoons butter, thyme, and cayenne. Process until smooth. Pour mixture into prepared pan.

Toss bread crumbs with remaining 2 tablespoons melted butter. Sprinkle crumbs over top of cheese mixture. Bake for 30 to 40 minutes, or until knife inserted in center comes out clean. Cool for 10 minutes before cutting into 1" squares. Serve warm or at room temperature.

Cheese squares can be made up to a day ahead and refrigerated. To reheat, arrange cut squares on baking sheet and warm in 350°F oven for 10 minutes.

*Process 3 slices of whole-grain bread in a food processor to make coarse crumbs. Spread crumbs on baking sheet and bake at 325°F for 10 minutes, until crisp.

Note: *You will need a food processor with at least an 11-cup capacity for this recipe.*

Crostini with Assorted Spreads

For crostini, slice narrow baguette-style loaves of bread into ½" slices. Arrange them on a baking sheet and toast under a broiler for 2 to 3 minutes per side, or bake them at 400°F for 12 to 15 minutes, turning slices over once. Serve crostini in a basket next to assorted spreads so guests can prepare their own. Alternately, arrange prepared crostini on a platter.

Gingered Shrimp and Crab Spread

1/3 cup mayonnaise

1/4 cup shredded fresh Parmesan cheese

1 tablespoon minced fresh ginger

1 tablespoon Dijon mustard

1 tablespoon lemon juice

8 oz. fresh or pasteurized cooked crabmeat, drained

1 can (4 oz.) tiny shrimp, drained

2 tablespoons snipped fresh cilantro

Pepper to taste

Makes 2 cups

Whisk together mayonnaise, cheese, ginger, mustard, and lemon juice. Stir in crab, shrimp, cilantro, and pepper. Cover and chill up to 1 day to allow flavors to blend.

Blue Cheese–Pecan Spread

8 oz. cream cheese, room temperature

4 oz. blue cheese, crumbled

1 tablespoon cognac or brandy

1/4 teaspoon dried thyme leaves

Dash cayenne

1/4 cup finely chopped toasted pecans*

Makes 1²/3 cups

Combine cheeses, cognac, thyme, and cayenne in a food processor. Process until smooth. Stir in pecans. (For a coarser spread, combine mixture with a fork.) Cover and chill up to 8 hours before serving.

*Toast pecans in a dry skillet over medium heat for 5 to 7 minutes, shaking pan occasionally.

Spinach Spread

5 cups cubed Italian bread, crusts removed

1/4 cup white wine vinegar

4 cups trimmed fresh spinach

3 tablespoons capers, drained

2 teaspoons anchovy paste

1 tablespoon Dijon mustard

1 to 2 cloves garlic, crushed

3 to 4 tablespoons olive oil

Salt to taste

Makes 2 cups

Toss bread with vinegar. Place in food processor. Add spinach, capers, anchovy paste, mustard, and garlic. Process until uniform. With processor running, add oil until spread is desired consistency. Add salt to taste.

Poached Shrimp with Olive Oil and Lemon Juice

2 lbs. fresh medium shrimp (30 to 35 count)

Poaching Liquid:

2 quarts water

1/4 cup white wine, or 2 tablespoons white wine vinegar

2 to 3 sprigs fresh parsley

1 carrot, cut into 2" pieces

1 stalk celery, cut into 2" pieces

2/3 cup extra virgin olive oil

1/2 cup fresh lemon juice

Salt and freshly ground pepper to taste

Makes 60 to 70 shrimp

Peel and devein shrimp, leaving tail on. Combine poaching liquid ingredients in a saucepan. Bring to a boil and simmer for 10 minutes. Add shrimp and cook for 2 to 3 minutes, or until shrimp is opaque. Drain and discard parsley, carrot, and celery.

Toss hot shrimp with olive oil, lemon juice, salt, and pepper. Let cool. Serve after marinating for 1 hour. Shrimp may be covered and chilled up to 1 day ahead. Bring shrimp to room temperature before serving for best flavor.

Note: *This recipe is easily doubled.*

Chili Turkey Tortillas

Filling:

2 turkey thighs (1¾ lbs.), skinned

1 small onion, quartered

1 clove garlic, crushed

½ teaspoon salt

½ teaspoon whole peppercorns

Water to cover

Chili Sauce:

4 dried New Mexico Red chiles

2 dried ancho chiles*

3 cups boiling water

1 teaspoon sugar

1 teaspoon salt

2 cloves garlic

¼ teaspoon ground cumin

3 pkgs. (8 oz. each) cream
cheese, softened

1 large red bell pepper, seeded
and cut into 3" slivers

12 green onions, cut into 3"
slivers

24 flour tortillas (6" diameter)

Makes 48 appetizers

Combine all filling ingredients in a large saucepan or Dutch oven. Bring to a boil over high heat. Cover. Reduce heat to medium-low. Simmer for 30 minutes, or until turkey is cooked and tender. Remove meat from broth. Let it cool, then remove meat from bones and shred.

Meanwhile, toast chiles for sauce in a dry skillet over medium heat until browned and slightly blistered. Let cool, then remove stems, seeds, and ribs from chiles. Tear chiles into pieces and place in a bowl. Cover with boiling water and let soak for 30 minutes. Drain and reserve 1 cup soaking liquid.

Place soaked chiles in blender with remaining sauce ingredients. Add reserved soaking liquid and process until smooth. Transfer to a saucepan. Simmer over medium heat for 15 to 20 minutes, or until thickened. Add shredded turkey. Cool completely. (Filling can be made a day ahead and refrigerated until ready to assemble tortillas.) Drain any excess liquid before assembling tortillas.

To assemble tortillas, spread 1 oz. cream cheese over a tortilla. Cut tortilla in half. Spoon 1 tablespoon filling down center of tortilla half and top with a few slivers of bell pepper and onions. Roll up tortilla half. Continue with remaining tortillas, cheese, filling, peppers, and onions. Serve within 4 hours of making tortillas.

*If ancho chiles are unavailable, use all New Mexico Red chiles for sauce.

Note: Wear rubber gloves when working with chiles.

Mini Mocha Tarts

Pastry:

1 cup all-purpose flour

1/2 cup powdered sugar

1/4 cup butter, chilled and diced

Pinch salt

2 to 3 tablespoons ice water

Filling:

2 cups semisweet chocolate pieces

1/2 cup heavy whipping cream

2 tablespoons instant espresso powder, or
   1/4 cup instant coffee granules

Makes 30 tarts

For pastry, combine flour, powdered sugar, butter, and salt in food processor. Process until mixture resembles coarse cornmeal. With motor running, drizzle in water, 1 tablespoon at a time, until dough clings and forms a ball. Wrap dough in plastic wrap, flatten into a disk, and chill for at least 30 minutes.

Heat oven to 400°F. Roll dough to 1/8" thickness. Cut out 30 rounds of dough using a 2 1/2" round cutter, rerolling dough scraps if necessary. Place dough circles in cups of mini-muffin tins. Prick bottom of tart crusts with fork. Bake for 8 to 10 minutes, or until golden brown. Cool crusts on wire racks. (Crusts may be made several days in advance and stored in an airtight container.)

For filling, combine chocolate, cream, and espresso powder in a small saucepan. Heat and stir over medium-low heat for 8 to 10 minutes, or until smooth. Remove from heat. Let stand for 10 minutes. Spoon 1 tablespoon filling into each tart crust. Cover with plastic wrap and chill up to 1 day before serving. Let tarts come to room temperature before serving.

Tipsy Pound Cake Tortes

Custard:

1/2 cup sugar

1/3 cup all-purpose flour

1/2 teaspoon salt

2 eggs

2 cups milk

2 tablespoons butter

1 teaspoon vanilla extract

Raspberry Filling:

2/3 cup seedless raspberry jam

2 teaspoons lemon juice

1/2 teaspoon grated orange peel

Apricot Filling:

1/3 cup apricot jam

1 teaspoon lemon juice

1/4 teaspoon grated orange peel

2 frozen pound cakes (10.75 oz. each)

1/2 cup dark rum

4 cups whipped cream

Makes 20 servings

For custard, combine sugar, flour, and salt in medium mixing bowl. Beat eggs at medium speed of electric mixer until thick and lemon colored. Set aside. Heat milk and butter in medium saucepan over medium heat until steaming. Gradually whisk hot milk into sugar mixture. Return to saucepan and cook over medium heat for 2 to 3 minutes, or until thickened, stirring constantly.

Gradually whisk hot mixture into eggs. Return to pan. Cook over medium heat for 4 to 6 minutes, or until thick and custard just starts to bubble, stirring constantly. Do not boil. Remove from heat. Stir in vanilla. Place custard in a bowl and cover with plastic wrap touching surface of custard. Chill.

In separate bowls, combine ingredients for raspberry and apricot fillings. Trim off tops of frozen pound cakes, then cut them crosswise to make 4 layers for each.

To assemble first torte, place bottom layer of cake in 8" × 4" loaf pan. Sprinkle with 1 tablespoon rum. Spread one-fourth of raspberry filling (about 3 tablespoons) over layer. Top with 1/3 cup custard. Place second layer over custard—don't press cake or custard will come out the sides. Sprinkle second layer with rum and top with half of the apricot filling and 1/3 cup custard.

Place third layer on top, sprinkle with 1 tablespoon rum, one-fourth of raspberry filling, and 1/3 cup custard. Top with remaining layer of cake and sprinkle that layer with 1 tablespoon rum. Cover with plastic wrap and chill. Repeat for second torte.

Chill tortes for several hours. Before serving, turn tortes out of loaf pans. Frost each torte with whipped cream. Carefully slice tortes with serrated knife and place on individual serving plates.

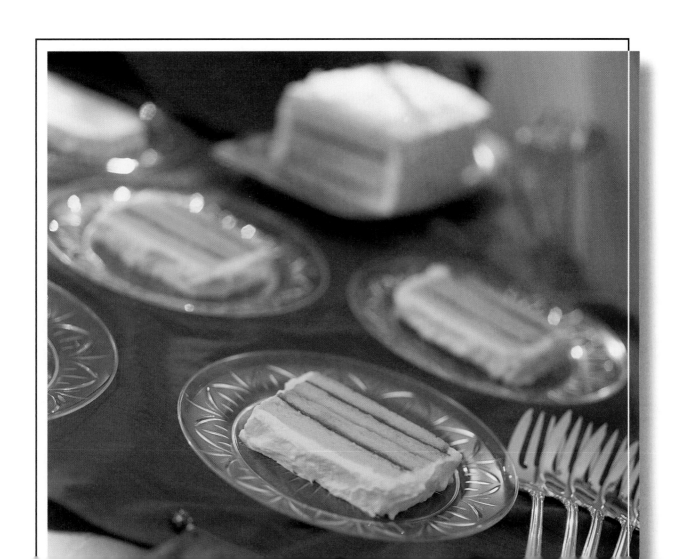

PLEASE COME
TO A
GARDEN SHOWER

garden shower

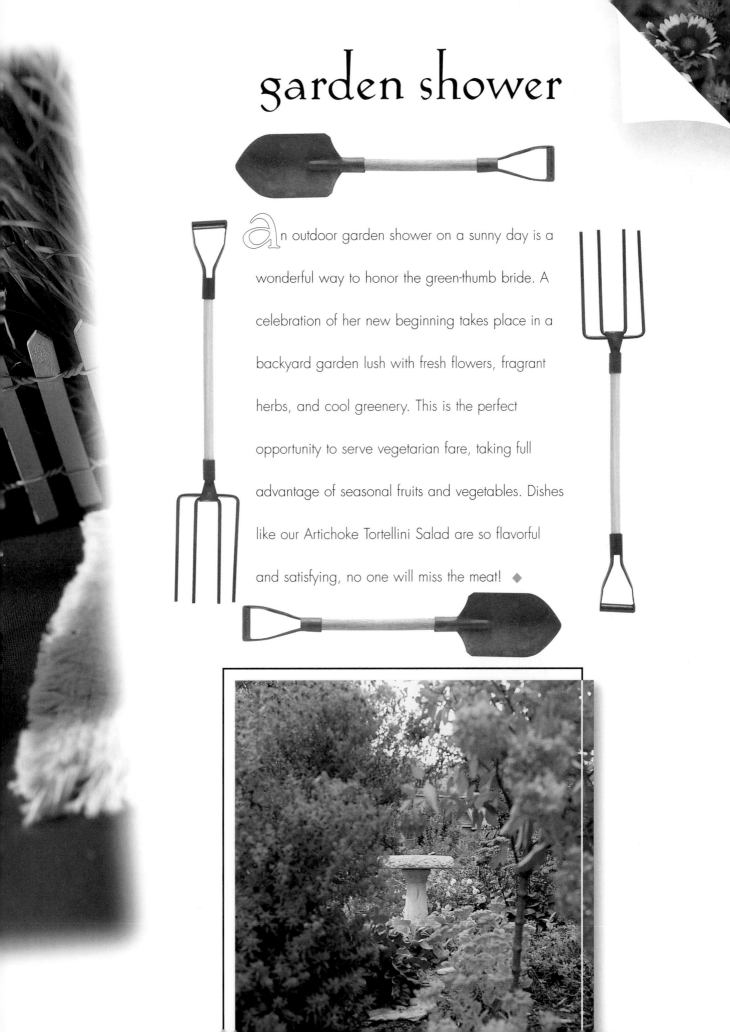

An outdoor garden shower on a sunny day is a wonderful way to honor the green-thumb bride. A celebration of her new beginning takes place in a backyard garden lush with fresh flowers, fragrant herbs, and cool greenery. This is the perfect opportunity to serve vegetarian fare, taking full advantage of seasonal fruits and vegetables. Dishes like our Artichoke Tortellini Salad are so flavorful and satisfying, no one will miss the meat! ◆

Glorious garden

surroundings require very little added

decoration. Slightly whimsical miniature

"lawn" centerpieces, gardening

paraphernalia serving double duty as

decorative accents and door prizes, and a

rustic garden cart filled with potted flowers

complement the outdoor stage. In harmony

with the decorating theme Mother Nature

has established, use woodsy natural

materials for embellishment: raffia, twine,

twigs, fresh and dried flowers, terra cotta,

tin, and wooden accents. ◆

We're throwing a backyard garden shower to honor Julia Anders.

When: Saturday, July 7, 2:00

Where: 5780 Garden Court

Given by: Char Gustavson

Julia is an avid gardener. Please bring a gift that will foster her green-thumb hobby.

Regrets only: 555-4201

PLEASE COME TO A **GARDEN SHOWER**

Perky picket fencing swings open to reveal the wheelbarrow full of flowers on the front of the garden shower invitation. Embossing is used to make the picket fence and the design behind it. Look for these or similar embossing plates at paper specialty shops. ◆

MATERIALS

- Sky-blue single-fold cards and envelopes
- Wheelbarrow and flowers (or similar design) embossing plate
- Picket fence embossing plate
- White cover-weight or card-weight paper for picket fence
- Watercolor markers
- Light box
- Stylus
- Glue
- White text-weight paper 8½″ × 11″ (21.8 × 28 cm) for inner message
- Deckle-blade scissors
- Packet of flower seeds

1 Position wheelbarrow embossing plate on front of card, so that picket fence embossing plate will cover wheelbarrow. Color in design areas, using watercolor markers.

2 Flip card and embossing plate over; place on light box. Emboss openings of plate.

3 Emboss a row of picket fencing, wide enough to cover card front. Cut out fence; cut in half. Glue sections to edges of card front.

4 Print out message on white paper, centering one message on each of four quadrants. Cut apart. Trim outer edges, using deckle-blade scissors. Glue to inside of card. Insert flower seed packet into invitation.

Leaning against the garden gate or a vine-covered arbor, this welcoming display of garden tools and accessories establishes the shower theme, and its components can double as door prizes! Featured items might include a stylish watering can, garden clogs, garden gloves, a gathering basket, and a broad-brimmed straw hat. ◆

Faux rusted tin shapes, available at craft stores, are personalized with paint-pen lettering. Jewelry pins are glued to the back for wearing. ◆

HINT
Prepare a few blank name pins, just in case one of the guests brings along an unexpected child or a dear friend who just dropped in from out of town.

Clever corsages, crafted from miniature garden tools, grace the bride-to-be and other guests of honor. Adorned with everlasting flowers (preserved or silk), these symbolic accessories become lasting mementos, perfect for displaying on a knickknack shelf or atop a potpourri bowl. ◆

ALTERNATIVE

Prepare a fresh flower corsage, following the directions for the herbal corsage (page 54). Use flowers from your garden, and attach them to the crossed tools instead of the artificial materials.

MATERIALS

- *Miniature hand trowel and fork*
- *Glue gun*
- *Jewelry pin*
- *Wire cutter*
- *Wrapped floral wire*
- *Silk greenery*
- *Thin twigs*
- *Two varieties of small preserved or silk flowers*
- *Large preserved or silk rose or other large blossom*
- *Small craft bug (butterfly, ladybug, dragonfly)*

1 Crisscross the trowel and fork, faceup; secure with hot glue. Glue the jewelry pin to the trowel back.

2 Wrap 12" (30.5 cm) floral wire twice around tools and through pin; twist together on front, leaving tails of equal length.

3 Arrange a few greenery sprigs and thin twigs in a fan shape over the tools; twist wire around them to secure. Trim wire tails.

4 Hot-glue rose over center of crossed tools. Glue smaller floral blossoms around rose. Glue bug onto tool handle.

Tailor-made for the task at hand and a suitable gift itself, a humble garden cart or wheelbarrow serves as a collection place for shower gifts. When it's time to open the gifts, the harvest can be easily wheeled over to the bride's chair! ◆

Nubby

natural-colored tablecloths have a homespun feel. Custom-made to fit ordinary card tables, the loosely woven fabric is simply fringed (page 142) around the outside edges. Along with the fresh green grass in the centerpiece, other bright accent colors liven up the party scene. As a uniting element, easy-to-make blue table runners crisscross the tables. ◆

MATERIALS

- Bright blue fabric
- Paper-backed fusible web, ½" to ¾" (1.3 to 2 cm) wide
- Iron and ironing board

1 Cut lengthwise strips of fabric 2" (5 cm) wider and longer than the desired finished width. Our strips are 13" (33 cm) wide and drop 13" (33 cm) from the table edge. Press under 1" (2.5 cm) hems along the table runner sides.

2 Unfold the hems. Fuse paper-backed fusible web to hem allowance, following manufacturer's instructions. Remove paper backing, refold hem, and fuse.

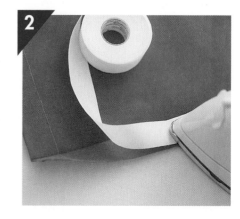

3 Repeat steps 1 and 2 for the runner ends.

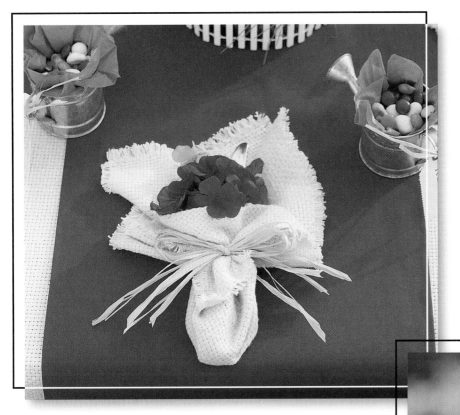

Fringed napkins are folded into a diagonal square with the top flap folded down (diagram). Flatware and a showy silk nosegay are tucked inside and tied with raffia. ◆

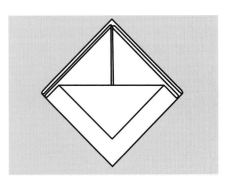

Pocket-size wooden bird houses, washed in primary colors, anchor the corners of the tablecloths. Each is hung from a button sewn to the fabric. ◆

Bright colors of tissue paper line miniature tin watering cans, transforming them into adorable nut cups. Each carries a raffia-tied nametag, reserving the guest's special place at the table. ◆

Miniature backyards,

complete with birdbaths and wildlife, adorn the centers of the tables. Painted signs hanging on mini picket fences carry lighthearted messages. ◆

MATERIALS

- *Clear plastic container, 8" to 10" (20.5 to 25.5 cm) in diameter*
- *Potting soil*
- *Wheat berry seeds, available from garden centers or health-food stores*
- *Small clay pot and saucer*
- *Hot glue gun*
- *Miniature craft bird*
- *Miniature picket fence, available from craft store*
- *Miniature blank sign*
- *Marker*

HINT

Plant a test sample of wheat grass two to three weeks before the shower to determine the exact number of days needed for germination and growth.

No Cats Allowed!

1 Trim plastic container down to a depth of about 1" (2.5 cm). Fill with potting soil; sprinkle densely with wheat berry seeds. Cover seeds lightly with soil; water daily. Keep moist, but not soaking. Seeds should sprout within three to five days and grow to a height of 3" (7.5 cm) within ten days.

2 Invert clay pot; hot-glue clay saucer to bottom of pot, to make mini bird bath. Glue mini bird on edge of saucer.

3 Place birdbath on lawn. Surround container with mini picket fence. Write a cute message on the sign (No Cats Allowed, Keep off the Grass, Fly-by Spa, Sara's Sit 'n' Sip) and hang it from the fence.

A trusty garden trug moonlights as a bread basket on the
buffet table. Likewise, wicker, terra-cotta, and stoneware pieces
can be functional as well as quaint. ◆

Charming

garden markers rise from galvanized containers full of wheat grass to identify the foods on the buffet table. Blank wooden signs are transformed into miniature chalkboards for labeling each delicious dish. ◆

MATERIALS

- Galvanized containers
- Plastic for lining containers
- Styrofoam®
- Potting soil
- Wheat berry seeds
- Blank wooden signs
- Acrylic craft paint in desired colors
- Masking tape
- Chalkboard paint
- Small craft bugs
- Hot glue gun
- Wood glue
- Flat garden marker stakes
- Calcium carbonate chalk

1 Cut Styrofoam to fit bottom of container and fill to within 1" (2.5 cm) of top. Line container with plastic; insert Styrofoam. Cover with soil to just below container rim.

2 Sprinkle densely with wheat berry seeds. Cover seeds lightly with soil; water daily.

3 Paint signs; allow to dry. Mask off narrow border. Spray with chalkboard paint, following manufacturer's instructions. Remove tape. Allow to dry completely.

4 Hot-glue bug to sign corner. Glue signs to stakes using wood glue. Write on signs with chalk. Insert into containers, pushing down securely into Styrofoam.

Fresh

potted flowers or herbs are fitting party favors for your guests. Small terra-cotta pots are stenciled with simple floral designs. A silk butterfly or dragonfly on a pick is inserted into each pot, and the entire collection is displayed in an antique garden cart, wagon, or small wheelbarrow. ◆

1 week or more ahead:
- Make grocery list.

2 days ahead:
- Get groceries.
- Make lemonade base.

1 day ahead:
- Prepare gazpacho; chill.
- Prepare salad; chill.
- Make shortbread portion of tart.

Morning of:
- Purchase fresh rolls.

2 hours before:
- Prepare sauce and berries for tart.
- Fill pitcher of water to make lemonade.

1 hour before:
- Prepare salad plates with salad.
- Fill bowls with gazpacho.

Just before serving:
- Fill ice bin for lemonade.
- Set out all food.
- Prepare individual servings of tart.

Artichoke Tortellini Salad

2 pkgs. (9 oz. each) refrigerated cheese tortellini

3 cans (13.75 oz. each) artichoke hearts, quartered

2 cups thinly sliced carrots

1 cup sliced celery

1 cup chopped red bell pepper

1 cup sliced pitted kalamata olives

1/2 cup sliced green onions

Dressing:

1/2 cup white wine vinegar

1/4 cup olive oil

2 tablespoons sugar

1 1/2 teaspoons dried oregano leaves

1 teaspoon dried basil leaves

1 teaspoon minced garlic

1 teaspoon salt

Freshly ground pepper to taste

Leaf lettuce

Shredded fresh Parmesan cheese

Makes 12 servings

Prepare pasta as directed on package. Rinse with cold water. Drain well. In large bowl, combine pasta with artichoke hearts, carrots, celery, bell pepper, olives, and onions. In measuring cup, whisk together dressing ingredients. Pour over pasta mixture; toss to coat. Chill up to 24 hours, stirring occasionally. Serve salad on lettuce-lined plates. Garnish with shredded Parmesan cheese.

Notes: Add 2 cups cubed cooked chicken or cooked shrimp to salad.

Substitute 3/4 cup prepared Italian vinaigrette for dressing in recipe.

HINT
Remove onion and garlic odors from your fingers by rubbing them over a stainless steel surface, such as the kitchen sink or a spoon.

Garden Gazpacho

4½ cups finely chopped seeded tomatoes

2½ cups finely chopped seeded cucumber, unpeeled

2½ cups finely chopped celery

2½ cups finely chopped yellow bell pepper, seeded

2/3 cup shredded carrots

1/3 cup finely chopped red or yellow onion

2 teaspoons minced garlic

2/3 cup torn rye or sourdough bread

1/3 cup loosely packed fresh basil

1/3 cup loosely packed fresh parsley

8 cups tomato juice or vegetable juice

½ cup red wine vinegar

2 tablespoons sugar

2 tablespoons olive oil

2 tablespoons fresh lemon juice

2 tablespoons Worcestershire sauce

1 to 2 teaspoons hot pepper sauce

Salt to taste

Makes 12 servings

In large bowl, combine tomatoes, cucumber, celery, bell pepper, carrots, onion, and garlic. In food processor, process bread, basil, and parsley until finely chopped. Add to vegetables with remaining ingredients. Chill up to 24 hours. Serve cold.

Shortbread layer:

1 cup all-purpose flour

1/4 cup sugar

2 teaspoons grated lemon peel

1 teaspoon baking powder

1/2 cup butter, cubed

1 egg, beaten

1/4 cup milk

1/2 teaspoon vanilla extract

Cheesecake layer:

2 1/2 pkgs. (8 oz. each) cream cheese, softened

1 1/4 cups sugar

1 egg

1 tablespoon lemon juice

2 teaspoons vanilla extract

1/2 cup currant jelly

4 cups berries (raspberries, sliced strawberries, blueberries)

Makes 12 servings

Glazed Berry Cheesecake Tart

Heat oven to 350°F. For shortbread layer, combine flour, sugar, lemon peel, and baking powder in medium bowl. Cut in butter until mixture resembles coarse crumbs. In small bowl, combine egg, milk, and vanilla. Add to flour mixture and stir just until mixture is combined. Spread in bottom of 9" × 13" baking pan. Set aside.

For cheesecake layer, beat cream cheese, sugar, egg, lemon juice, and vanilla together at medium speed of electric mixer until smooth and creamy. Spread over shortbread layer in pan. Bake for 30 to 35 minutes, or until golden. Cool completely on wire rack. Cover and chill up to 24 hours.

Heat currant jelly in small saucepan over medium-low heat until smooth, whisking constantly. Remove from heat and let cool. Pour over berries, stirring gently to coat. Spoon over individual servings of tart just before serving.

Old-Fashioned Lemonade

3½ cups water

1¾ cups sugar

1¾ cups fresh lemon juice, strained
(6 to 7 lemons)

6 cups ice water

Ice

Lemon slices for garnish

Makes 12 servings

In a medium saucepan, heat water and sugar over medium heat until sugar is dissolved, stirring constantly. Remove from heat and let cool for 15 minutes. Stir in lemon juice. Pour lemonade base into covered pitcher and chill.

For each serving, combine ½ cup lemonade base with ½ cup ice water in a tall glass. Fill glass with ice and garnish with lemon slice.

Notes: *Lemonade base can be made up to three days in advance.*

For a lemonade punch, substitute soda water for ice water and add a scoop of lemon sherbet instead of the ice.

gourmet
dinner shower

Couples and mixed singles gather for an

enjoyable evening of cooking, socializing, and

showering gifts on their soon-to-be-wed friends.

Especially suited to a couple who enjoys preparing

and eating fine food, a gourmet shower, at which

the guests prepare the meal, gives everyone a

chance to play the role of chef for an evening.

With careful planning by the party hosts,

even novice cooks join in the fun and take an

active part in the meal preparation. ◆

The kitchen

is a bustling hub of activity for

this party, with workstations set up

for each cooking duo. The menu

is carefully planned out so that

sink, stove, oven, and grill will be

utilized at different times to avoid

congestion. The casual, genial

atmosphere encourages easy,

lighthearted conversation, while the

guests, hosts, and honorees pool

their culinary talents to create a

fabulous meal. ◆

Hand-delivered

wine bottles wrapped with invitations to a gourmet dinner shower are a unique party favor as well. ◆

MATERIALS

- Heavy, sturdy paper for outer wrap
- Seven small grommets, awl, and grommet setting tool
- 8½" × 11" (21.8 × 28 cm) text-weight paper for inner message
- Glue
- Cover-weight paper for address tags
- Narrow leather lacing
- Recipe cards

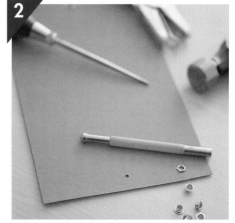

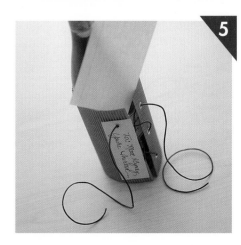

1 Cut a rectangle of heavy paper with the length equal to the circumference of the wine bottle and the width equal to the height of the straight part of the bottle, about 5½" (14 cm). Mark locations for grommets ½" (1.3 cm) from short ends, with top and bottom marks 1" (2.5 cm) from paper edge and third mark centered between them.

2 Make holes slightly smaller than grommets at marks, using awl. Place grommets on hard, flat work surface; press paper facedown over grommets. Set grommets using special tool.

3 Print out shower message on text-weight paper; two messages to a sheet, turned in landscape direction. Cut in half; trim ends to fit inside outer wrap. Glue in place.

4 Cut small tag from cover-weight paper. Set grommet in one end. Address tag.

5 Cut leather lacing about 40" (102 cm) long. Lace through grommets from bottom up. Wrap invitation around bottle; slip recipe card inside. Tie snugly, securing address tag behind bow.

Cooking utensils and herbs, cleverly arranged in a wall basket, make an intriguing entry display, setting the lighthearted tone for the party. ◆

MATERIALS

- Wicker wall basket, at least 6" (15 cm) deep
- Kitchen towel
- Styrofoam®, 2" (5 cm) thick
- Plastic cups for transplanting herbs
- Two or three small potted herbs of different leaf size, height, and texture
- Assorted wooden and metal cooking utensils
- Excelsior or Spanish moss

1 Fanfold the towel; drape it over the basket bottom, extending a short distance over the basket rim in the front and longer in the back. Fan out the folds.

2 Cut Styrofoam to fit basket bottom; wedge in place over towel. Position plastic cups to fit in basket, allowing at least 1" (2.5 cm) space at back; press into foam to desired height. Transplant herbs into plastic cups; place in basket.

3 Arrange utensils behind herbs; press handles into foam. Cover any exposed foam with excelsior.

$\mathcal{A}$n herbal corsage and boutonniere distinguish the honored couple. Tiny utensils add a touch of whimsy. ◆

MATERIALS

- Pompom chrysanthemums or similar small, compact flowers
- 24-gauge floral stem wires, cut in half
- Floral tape
- Two or three fresh herbs in different leaf sizes and textures
- Miniature utensils
- Wire cutter
- Ribbon
- Corsage pins

1 Cut flower stem 1" (2.5 cm) below head. Bend one end of stem wire into small hook. Pierce center top of flower with straight end of wire, and push wire down through flower and stem until hook disappears inside flower.

2 Wrap stem and wire with floral tape, beginning as close to flower head as possible. Stretch tape gently as you wrap, pressing tape onto itself. Warmth of fingers softens paraffin in tape, causing it to stick. Prepare as many flowers as desired.

3 Bend a wire in half; slip over herb stem at point ⅔ of the way from bottom of stem. Wrap doubled wire together with herb stem, using floral tape, as in step 2. Prepare as many herb stems as desired.

4 Layer two herb stems; place flower over herbs, allowing herbs to extend above flower head. Wrap tape around all stems twice.

5 Twist wire around utensil handle. Place over other stems; wrap tape around all twice. Add more herb and flower stems as desired; wrapping twice with each addition. Continue in this manner to desired size.

6 Wrap all stems together to just below last flower. Cut wires; wrap tape over ends. Tie ribbon below last flower.

Colorful aprons for gals and guys wait to be chosen by the guests. Hidden inside the pocket of each apron is a miniature utensil that identifies the portion of the meal the wearer will prepare. Each guest is partnered with another who selects an apron with a matching utensil. Aprons can be gathered from your own collection, from friends and relatives, or from thrift stores. Others can be easily sewn using simple patterns. ◆

Neatly laminated recipes are held by ingenious props made from potted herbs and miniature clothespins. Recipes can be photocopied from pages 63, 64, and 67 and laminated for protection. ◆

MATERIALS

- *Photocopying machine; card-weight paper*
- *Paper laminating product*
- *Potted herbs*
- *Hot glue gun or craft glue*
- *Small clothespins*
- *Wired ribbon*
- *Flat wooden stakes*

1 Photocopy the recipes. Laminate the pages, following the manufacturer's directions. Cut apart.

2 Glue clothespins to ends of wooden stakes. Insert into potted herbs.

3 Tie stakes with ribbons. Secure recipes to tops of stakes with clothespins.

Table runners are kitchen

towels linked end-to-end with simple button and raffia "frogs." Raffia is wrapped and tied in a figure eight around mix-and-match buttons, sewn near the towel edges. Colors of towels and buttons are selected to represent the season and establish a theme for the table decor. ◆

Homespun dish-

cloths, lily-folded and tucked inside chunky goblets, suffice as napkins for the event. ◆

1 Fold napkin in half diagonally, with open corners at the top.

2 Fold right and left points up from center of fold, so that points are even with, but slightly to sides of, center points.

3 Fold bottom point up to 1" (2.5 cm) below center. Accordion-pleat napkin from side to side.

4 Place in glass and spread out points.

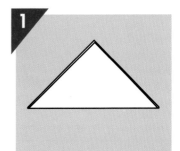

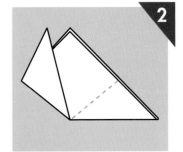

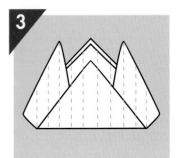

A̶romatic infusing balls, filled with mulling spices or simmering potpourri, rest in the center of the napkins as party favors. Polymer clay leaves imprinted with the guests' names serve as place cards. Any shape, suitable to your party theme, can be used.◆

MATERIALS

- *Polymer clay, such as Sculpey® or Fimo®, in leaf colors*
- *Rolling pin*
- *Leaf-shaped cookie cutters*
- *Small screw eyes*
- *Polyester batting*
- *Baking sheet*
- *Metallic paint pens*
- *Infusing balls*
- *Mulling spices*

1 Manipulate clay, following manufacturer's directions. Roll to ¼" (6 mm) thickness. Cut out shapes with cookie cutters. Insert screw eye in stem end.

2 Place batting on baking sheet. Place leaf shapes on batting. Bake according to manufacturer's directions. Allow to cool completely.

3 Write guests' names on leaves, using metallic paint pens. Attach to infuser chains. Fill infusers with spices.

Fresh and colorful vegetables, seasonal flowers, and herbs are artfully arranged in copper colanders as the centerpiece for the dining table. Floral foam for fresh flowers is soaked in water and placed in a bowl inside the colander for inserting the mums and holding the candle. Other items can be speared with floral wire or picks to hold them in place. ◆

Candlelight glows warmly through peppers that are finely carved with leaf designs. ◆

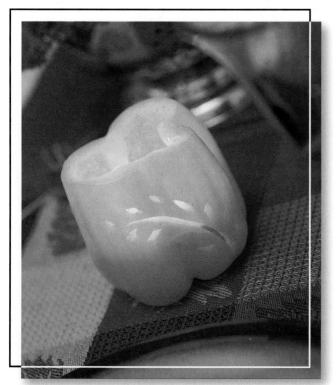

MATERIALS

- *Peppers in desired colors. Look for broad evenly shaped "shoulders," as peppers must stand upside down.*
- *Spoon*
- *Pencil*
- *Craft knife*
- *Tea light candles*

1 Carefully remove stem. Cut round or shaped opening from bottom of pepper. Scoop out inside with spoon; create flat area for placing tea light.

2 Lightly score design on outside of pepper with pencil. (Multiple small slit openings are more attractive than large designs.) Cut openings with craft knife.

3 Store carved peppers in sealed bag in refrigerator until just before the party. Insert candles; light just before seating.

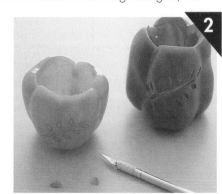

Whimsical wedding attire, worn by the salt shaker and pepper mill, add a dash of humor to the affair. "Please pass the happy couple!" ◆

MATERIALS

- Salt shaker and pepper mill
- Tulle or bridal illusion, for veil
- ½ yard (0.5 m) satin ribbon, ⅛" (3 mm) wide
- Hand needle or sewing machine; white thread
- Hot glue or craft glue
- Satin flower trim for bride's bouquet
- Dark felt or synthetic suede scrap, for tux
- Tiny ribbon bow, for bow tie
- Tiny flower, for boutonniere

HINT
If secured with hot glue, items can be easily removed by placing the shaker and mill in the freezer for a short time.

1 Cut tulle in oval shape about 15" × 8" (38 × 20.5 cm). Fold crosswise so one edge is 1" (2.5 cm) longer than the other. Place ribbon inside fold. Stitch alongside ribbon to form casing.

2 Tie ribbon around salt shaker head, forming bow at front; gather veil toward back. Trim ribbon ends as desired. Glue small satin rose to center of salt shaker for bride's bouquet.

3 Measure circumference of pepper mill. Cut a rectangle of felt or suede with this width and desired length for tuxedo. Round front corners of tux; cut small notch in center of bottom edge.

4 Wrap tux around pepper mill; secure with hot glue. Attach bow tie and tiny boutonniere.

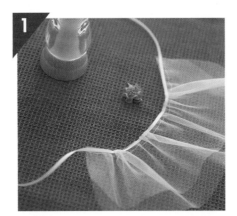

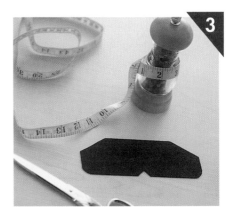

Polaroid party snapshots, favorite recipes collected from the guests, and notes of congratulations and best wishes, make a fitting memento for the engaged couple. A small blank scrapbook, available at craft and paper supply stores, is decorated to reflect the party theme. A handy Velcro® closure works to hold the covers apart to stand easel-style for propping recipes. ◆

MATERIALS

- *Spiral-bound mini memory book, 4¼" × 5½" (10.8 × 14 cm)*
- *Rubber stamps with cooking theme; ink*
- *Decorative papers, gel pens as desired*
- *Narrow ribbon*
- *Craft glue*
- *Adhesive-backed Velcro® dot*
- *Mini Polaroid camera and film*
- *Page protectors, optional*

CUSTOMS

Herbs, because of their real or imagined powers, carry symbolic meanings: rosemary for remembrance, myrtle for true love, sage for health, thyme for courage, parsley for festivity, sweet basil for good wishes, chamomile for energy, fennel for strength, lavender for luck, lemon verbena for unity, marjoram for joy, mint for virtue.

1 Stamp desired images on front cover of memory book, with spiral binding at the top. Embellish with decorative papers, if desired.

2 Cut 4" (10 cm) strip of ribbon. Fold under ½" (1.3 cm) at each end; glue. Tie small bow with remaining ribbon; glue to one end of ribbon strip. Adhere loop side of Velcro dot to back side of opposite end.

3 Glue ribbon with bow to front cover near lower edge. Wrap ribbon over edge to back. Adhere hook side of Velcro dot to cover back, aligning it to ribbon end.

4 Insert guests' favorite recipes and mini snapshots taken during the party into the book, reserving at least two facing pages for each guest. Allow room for guests to write personal wishes for the bride and groom. Cover pages with page protectors, if desired.

Schedule

1 week or more ahead:
- Make grocery list.

1 day ahead:
- Get groceries.

Morning of:
- Set up workstations with appropriate measuring tools, bowls, etc.; set out nonperishable ingredients.
- Make up trays with refrigerated ingredients for each recipe; chill (if desired, some ingredients could be chopped, shredded, etc., ahead of time).
- Prepare grill; do not light.

Meal Preparation

1½ to 2 hours before dinner:
- Roast peppers under broiler first (if desired, roast ahead of time in the morning).
- Make cake.
- Prepare gnocchi; do not cook.
- Light grill.
- Make mayo for appetizers.
- Make salad.

1 hour before:
- Grill portabellas and pitas first.
- Prepare appetizers; serve immediately (nibble and cook).
- Stuff and grill steaks.
- Whip cream for cake.

½ hour before:
- Roast zucchini.
- Cook gnocchi; toss with butter.

Just before serving:
- Set out salad, gnocchi, and roasted peppers and zucchini.
- Slice steaks.
- Prepare wedges of cake with whipped cream.

> ### HINT
> Freshly ground pepper from a pepper mill is much tastier than ground pepper from a tin can, not to mention the bit of class it adds to your table.

Portabella Pita Appetizers

INGREDIENTS

6 portabella mushroom caps, 4" to 5" in
    diameter

1 1/2 cups Italian vinaigrette

1/4 cup olive oil

6 soft pita loaves, 6" in diameter

Chili-Garlic Mayonnaise:

3/4 cup mayonnaise

1 1/2 teaspoons chili powder

1 1/2 teaspoons lemon juice

1 teaspoon minced garlic,
    or 1/4 teaspoon garlic powder

Salt to taste

6 cups baby salad greens

1/3 cup Italian vinaigrette

3/4 cup crumbled Gorgonzola cheese

Makes 12 servings

Prepare grill for medium direct heat. Brush tops and bottoms of mushroom caps with 1 1/2 cups vinaigrette. Let stand for 15 minutes.

Brush both sides of pitas with olive oil. Combine mayonnaise, chili powder, lemon juice, garlic, and salt; set Chili-Garlic Mayonnaise aside. Toss greens with remaining 1/3 cup vinaigrette.

Grill mushrooms for 3 to 5 minutes per side, or just until tender. Grill pitas for 2 to 3 minutes per side, until browned. Slice mushroom caps into strips. Spread Chili-Garlic Mayonnaise evenly over hot pitas. Top each with 1 cup greens, 1 sliced mushroom cap, and 2 tablespoons cheese. Cut pitas into wedges. Serve immediately.

Permission granted by publisher to photocopy this page.

Grilled Garlic Steaks

INGREDIENTS

2 boneless beef top loin or top sirloin steaks,
    2" thick, about 2 1/2 lbs. each

1 tablespoon olive oil

1 cup chopped green onions

1/4 cup minced garlic

1/2 cup snipped fresh flat-leaf parsley

1 1/2 teaspoons salt, divided

1 teaspoon freshly ground pepper

Makes 12 servings

Trim steaks. Cut a pocket in the side of each steak starting 1/2" from one edge and cutting horizontally to within 1/2" of each side. Set aside.

Heat oil in small skillet over medium-low heat. Add onions and garlic. Sauté for 8 to 9 minutes, or until tender but not browned. Stir in parsley and 1/2 teaspoon salt. Stuff steaks evenly with herb mixture. Secure pockets shut with wooden picks. Season

steaks with remaining salt and pepper. Set aside.

Prepare grill for medium direct heat. Grill steaks, covered, for 35 to 40 minutes, or until medium rare (internal temperature reads 140°F), turning occasionally. Remove from grill. Cover. Let stand for 10 minutes. Remove and discard wooden picks. Slice steaks or cut into serving-size pieces for serving.

Spinach Gnocchi

INGREDIENTS

2 pkgs. (10 oz. each) frozen
   chopped spinach, thawed

1/2 cup finely chopped onion

2 tablespoons butter

1 cup grated Parmesan cheese

1 1/3 cups whole-milk ricotta cheese

2 eggs

1/2 teaspoon salt

Dash ground nutmeg

1 1/3 cups all-purpose flour

4 to 6 tablespoons butter, melted

Makes about 120 gnocchi

Cook spinach according to package directions. Drain well in fine-mesh sieve, pressing with back of spoon to remove as much liquid as possible. Place spinach in large mixing bowl. Set aside.

In small skillet, sauté onion in 2 tablespoons butter over medium heat for 3 to 5 minutes, or until onion is tender. Add onion to spinach with cheeses, eggs, salt, and nutmeg. Mix well. Stir in flour.

Drop heaping teaspoons of spinach mixture on lightly floured surface. With lightly floured hands, roll pieces of spinach mixture into balls. Indent each piece with a finger.

Bring a large pot of salted water to a gentle boil. Cook gnocchi in batches for 3 to 5 minutes, until they float. Remove with slotted spoon and drain. Toss hot gnocchi with melted butter just before serving.

Permission granted by publisher to photocopy this page.

Orange-Fennel Salad

INGREDIENTS

Dressing:

1/2 cup olive oil

2 tablespoons orange juice

2 tablespoons white wine vinegar

2 teaspoons dried oregano leaves

1/2 teaspoon salt

12 cups baby salad greens or torn romaine
   lettuce

2 large fennel bulbs, cut into thin strips

1 large red onion, halved lengthwise then
   thinly sliced

1 cup slivered pitted kalamata olives

6 oranges, peeled and cut into thin rounds

Freshly ground pepper to taste

Freshly grated Parmesan cheese to taste

Makes 12 servings

In small bowl, whisk oil, orange juice, vinegar, oregano, and salt together. In large bowl, combine greens, fennel, onion, and olives. Add dressing. Toss to coat.

Arrange orange slices on salad plates. Mound greens mixture on top. Garnish with pepper and Parmesan.

Note: *Alternately, peeled oranges may be coarsely cut up and tossed with other salad ingredients.*

Roasted Peppers and Zucchini

INGREDIENTS

2 large red bell peppers

2 large yellow bell peppers

6 medium zucchini

1/4 cup olive oil

2 tablespoons balsamic vinegar

Salt to taste

Freshly ground pepper to taste

Makes 12 servings

Under a broiler or on a grill, roast peppers for 8 to 10 minutes, or until blackened and blistered, turning occasionally. Place peppers in paper or plastic bag for 10 minutes to steam. Remove stems, seeds, and skin. Cut peppers into 1" strips. Set aside at room temperature.

Heat oven to 400°F. Cut zucchini diagonally into 1/4" slices. Toss with olive oil to coat. Spread on baking sheet. Roast for 14 to 16 minutes, or just until tender. Arrange zucchini on platter with roasted peppers. Drizzle with vinegar. Sprinkle with salt and pepper to taste. Serve immediately or at room temperature.

Note: *If desired, use all red bell peppers and substitute yellow summer squash for some or all of the zucchini.*

Permission granted by publisher to photocopy this page.

Bittersweet Chocolate-Pumpkin Cake

INGREDIENTS

1 1/2 cups all-purpose flour

1/3 cup unsweetened cocoa

1 1/2 teaspoons baking powder

1 teaspoon baking soda

1/2 teaspoon ground cinnamon

1/2 teaspoon salt

3 eggs

3/4 cup granulated sugar

3/4 cup brown sugar

1 can (15 oz.) pumpkin purée

3/4 cup vegetable oil

1 teaspoon vanilla extract

4 oz. bittersweet or semisweet chocolate, finely chopped*

Cinnamon Whipped Cream:

1/4 cup sugar

1/4 teaspoon ground cinnamon

1 1/2 cups heavy whipping cream

1 teaspoon vanilla extract

Makes 12 servings

Heat oven to 350°F. Spray two 8" round cake pans with nonstick vegetable cooking spray. Line the bottom of each pan with a circle of parchment paper. Set pans aside.

Into a medium bowl, sift flour, cocoa, baking powder, baking soda, cinnamon, and salt. In a large bowl, beat eggs and sugars at medium speed of electric mixer until creamy. Add pumpkin, oil, and vanilla. Beat until smooth. Add flour mixture; mix well. Stir in chocolate.

Pour batter evenly into prepared pans. Bake for 35 to 40 minutes, or until a wooden pick inserted in the center comes out clean. Let cakes cool in pans for 15 minutes. Turn

cakes out onto wire racks, remove parchment paper, and cool completely.

For whipped cream, combine sugar and cinnamon in large bowl. Add cream and vanilla. Beat at medium-high speed of electric mixer until cream holds soft peaks. Serve immediately or refrigerate until serving time. Top wedges of cake with dollop of Cinnamon Whipped Cream.

If desired, use miniature chocolate chips instead of chopped chocolate.

bridesmaids' tea party

tradition and ceremony accompany the bridesmaids' tea party, held in the last two weeks before the wedding. A pink color theme imparts a feminine, romantic atmosphere for girl talk, fancy food, and a proper cup of tea. While the bride hosts this party, her honor attendant pours the tea and may help with the arrangements. The bride honors each attendant with a personal gift—often a piece of jewelry to wear for the wedding. In turn, the bridesmaids together give the bride a significant gift—perhaps something old, something new, something borrowed, or something blue! ◆

Refined and

tasteful, an afternoon tea party is

a classy, intimate affair. In a

secluded open-air location, filled

with luxuriant greenery and

fragrant flowers, the bride and

her bridesmaids relax, share

dreams, and pamper themselves.

With seating arranged around

small, exquisitely appointed tables,

conversation flows easily and

each guest shares equally in the

party limelight. ◆

Dainty and feminine, this tea-bag invitation is a fitting way to invite the bridesmaids to their special celebration. The handwritten message reflects the very personal theme for this girls-only gathering. ◆

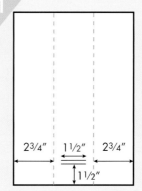

MATERIALS

- Translucent pink or white vellum, 8½" × 11" (21.8 × 28 cm)
- Craft knife; cutting board
- Scallop-blade scissors
- Decorative pink paper
- Fine decorative cord

- Stapler
- Small purchased or handmade envelopes, at least 3" × 4" (7.5 × 10 cm)
- Pressed flowers, optional

1 Fold in one long edge of the vellum 2¾" (7 cm). Repeat with the other side. Open folds. Cut two 1½" (3.8 cm) slits, ¼" (6 mm) apart, 1½" (3.8 cm) from bottom of center section.

2 Fold lower section under 4" (10 cm); crease. Fold invitation back in opposite directions ½" (1.3 cm) on either side of last fold; crease.

3 Fold top section down at point even with open edges; crease. Cut away two inner folds of top flap. Cut top flap to a point, using scallop-blade scissors.

4 Cut two rectangles of decorative paper to fit easily into front and back pockets. Handwrite message on plain side of one rectangle. Cut 5" (12.5 cm) piece of cord; knot both ends. Staple to center top of message. Insert message into back pocket; insert blank paper into front pocket, decorative side facing outward. Insert pressed flowers into pockets, if desired. Fold flap closed; insert through slits.

Elegant pink rose topiaries greet the guests and establish the feminine, sophisticated theme of the bridesmaids' tea party. Made with long-stemmed silk roses and silk ivy, these everlasting topiaries can be used again, perhaps at the ceremony or reception entrance. ◆

MATERIALS

- Decorative container
- Stones or marbles
- Styrofoam®
- Sturdy straight branch, ½" (1.3 cm) diameter, same length as roses
- 5 long-stemmed silk rose clusters
- Floral wire
- Silk ivy garland
- Moss
- Sheer ribbon

1 Weight the bottom of the container with stones or marbles. Cut Styrofoam to fit inside the container; wedge the foam tightly into container. Insert branch deep into center of foam.

2 Insert rose stems into foam, working in a tight circle around the branch. Twist stems around branch; wrap stems and branch together with floral wire just below flower heads.

3 Wind ivy garland in and around flower heads and partway down stems. Cover exposed foam with moss. Tie large bow with long flowing tails, just under flower heads.

Lush ferns, baskets of flowers, and billowing pink ribbon streamers decorate the scene. Arriving guests are greeted with refreshing glasses of chilled pink lemonade. ◆

Wedding photos from generations past stand in antique frames on a lace-covered side table. Pink roses arranged in an heirloom vase enhance the nostalgic display. ◆

Sumptuous table linens set the stage for a lovely tea party. Gentle swags are pinned up in the table topper edge and are accented with ribbon bows. ◆

MATERIALS

- Floor-length round white tablecloth
- Round pink tablecloth, about 2/3 the length of larger cloth
- Large safety pins
- Wide ribbon

1 Divide the top tablecloth circumference into equal sections, one for each place setting; mark. Gather the edge to within 4" (10 cm) of the table edge, using a large safety pin, inserted from the wrong side; repeat at each mark.

2 Secure a large ribbon bow with streamers at each pin.

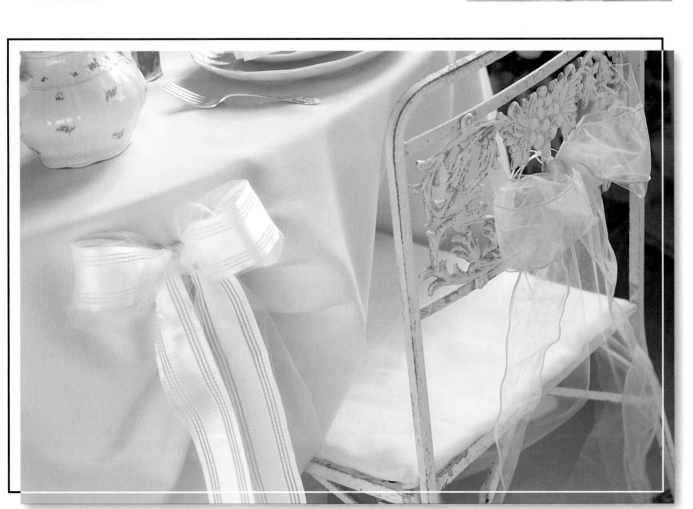

Sheer pink ribbons tied in gossamer bows with flowing streamers transform ordinary chairs into seats of distinction. ◆

Pink linen napkins are simply fanfolded and tied
with sheer pink ribbons. ◆

Delicate china plates, teacups, and saucers in matched or
mismatched patterns add to the Victorian ambiance. ◆

Fresh rosebud topiaries serve as place cards and favors. With daily watering, they may last up to the day of the wedding. ◆

MATERIALS

- Floral foam for fresh flowers
- Small brass containers
- Small pink roses, five to seven per topiary
- Floral tape
- Moss
- Sheer pink ribbon
- Pink card stock or precut paper place cards

1 Cut floral foam to fit tightly inside each container. Submerge foam in water until thoroughly saturated. Place foam in containers.

2 Cut rose stems to uniform length, 6" to 8" (15 to 20.5 cm). Insert five to seven stems upright into each container, working from the center outward. Wrap stems together with floral tape just below flower heads.

3 Cover foam with moss. Tie a ribbon bow with flowing tails just under flower heads. Print name on card stock rectangle; punch small hole in one corner, and tie onto stems.

HINT
Prepare the topiaries, following steps 1 and 2, a day or two before the party, and store them loosely wrapped in plastic in the refrigerator. Add the ribbon and place cards just before the party.

Dainty pink handcrafted boxes hint of the extreme care taken in selecting the gifts held inside. Though intricate in appearance, the boxes are easy to make, using purchased templates and simple cutting and folding skills. ◆

MATERIALS

- Box template in desired size and shape, available in craft stores or paper specialty stores
- Pink card-weight or cover-weight paper; one 8½″ × 11″ (21.8 × 28 cm) sheet per box
- Removable tape
- Light box or other illuminated glass surface
- Stylus
- Fine-tip dimensional white pen
- Craft glue (optional)
- Small-hole paper punch
- Narrow sheer ribbon, white or pink

1 Secure box template to right side of paper, using removable tape. Secure, template side down, to light box or other illuminated glass surface. Emboss openings with stylus.

2 Remove template. Cut out box along outside lines and any other lines indicated on the template. On right side, embellish cover and sides of box with tiny dot pattern, using dimensional white pen. Allow to dry completely.

3 Fold all inside lines toward the center, forming box. Insert any tabs as indicated; secure with glue, if desired. Insert gift.

4 Cut a small rectangle of scrap paper for gift tag; write name on tag. Punch a hole in one corner for attaching to ribbon. Tie box closed with narrow ribbon.

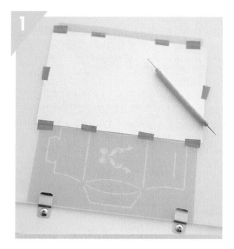

Mystic petits fours, served as the grand finale to the event, hold secret fortune-telling powers. Arranged on tiered plates in the center of the table, they are the focus of attention and conversation throughout the party. A symbolic charm, hidden between the cake papers of each serving, has special meaning for the lucky recipient—a heart foretells new love; a ring predicts the next to marry; a coin means good fortune; a key represents opportunity. Good luck may be symbolized by a four-leaf clover, a horseshoe, or a unicorn; a star might suggest fame; a butterfly new beginning. Follow the recipe and directions for decorating the petits fours on pages 84 and 85. ◆

Up to 1 week ahead:
- Make grocery list.
- Make rolls and freeze.
- Make Thyme-Vermouth Butter for beans and freeze.

2 days ahead:
- Get groceries.

1 day ahead:
- Make petits fours.
- Slice pats of Thyme-Vermouth Butter; re-freeze.

Morning of:
- Thaw rolls.
- Clean green beans.
- Assemble elements for making a pot of tea.
- Make salad.

2 hours before:
- Place salads on serving plates; chill until serving time.

1 hour before:
- Brown chicken, then bake.
- Prepare rice blend for chicken as directed on package.

1/2 hour before:
- Cook green beans.
- Prepare sauce for chicken.
- Warm plates.

Just before serving:
- Prepare individual serving plates with rice, chicken, sauce, garnishes, beans, and butter pats.
- Set out salad.
- Prepare tea; set out milk, lemon slices, and honey.

Green Beans with Thyme–Vermouth Butter

Thyme-Vermouth Butter:

2 tablespoons finely chopped shallots

1 teaspoon olive oil

1/2 cup butter, softened

1/2 teaspoon dried thyme leaves

2 tablespoons dry vermouth

1 lb. fresh green beans, trimmed

Makes 8 servings

For butter, sauté shallots in oil over medium-low heat for 8 to 10 minutes, or until shallots are golden. Remove from heat; cool completely. In small bowl, combine shallots, butter, and thyme. Stir in vermouth, 1 tablespoon at a time.

Spoon butter onto sheet of plastic wrap. Shape into a 6" log by rolling the wrap around butter. Twist ends of wrap tightly and freeze log.

Leave beans whole. Place in large saucepan with 2 cups water. Bring to a boil over medium-high heat. Cover. Reduce heat to medium. Simmer for 15 to 20 minutes, or just until tender. Drain. Top individual servings of beans with a small pat of butter.

Note: *Butter can be made up to a month ahead if overwrapped with foil and stored in the freezer.*

8 boneless skinless chicken breast halves
   (4 to 6 oz. each)
1 tablespoon dried herbes de Provence*
1/2 teaspoon seasoned salt
1/2 teaspoon freshly ground pepper
3 tablespoons olive oil
1/4 cup chicken broth
1/4 cup dry white wine

Sauce:
1/4 cup butter
1/3 cup all-purpose flour
1 1/2 cups chicken broth
1/2 cup half-and-half
1/4 cup dry white wine
Salt and pepper to taste

Hot cooked wild rice blend**
Snipped fresh parsley
Grated lemon peel

Makes 8 servings

Herbed Chicken

Heat oven to 350°F. Sprinkle both sides of chicken breasts evenly with herbes de Provence, salt, and pepper. Heat oil in large nonstick skillet over medium-high heat. Add breasts to skillet and cook for 3 to 5 minutes per side, or until browned. Place breasts in baking dish. Add 1/4 cup broth and 1/4 cup wine. Cover with foil. Bake for 15 to 30 minutes, or until chicken is no longer pink inside.

Meanwhile, make sauce. Melt butter in a small saucepan over medium heat. Whisk in flour. Cook for 2 minutes, whisking constantly. Remove roux from heat. In a medium saucepan, heat broth, half-and-half, and wine over medium-high heat until simmering. Reduce heat to medium-low. Whisk in roux a little at a time until completely incorporated. Add salt and pepper to taste. Keep sauce warm over medium-low heat until ready to serve, whisking occasionally.

Serve chicken breast on bed of hot cooked wild rice blend. Top with sauce and garnish with snipped fresh parsley and grated lemon peel.

*Herbes de Provence is a dried herb blend from southern France. If desired, use your favorite herb blend in its place.

**Use a packaged wild rice blend and prepare as directed on package.

Strawberry-Orange Poppy Seed Salad

6 oranges, peeled and sectioned

2 cups sliced strawberries

1 small red onion, thinly sliced and separated into rings

Dressing:

1/4 cup vegetable oil

1/4 cup honey

2 tablespoons fresh orange juice

1 tablespoon white wine vinegar

1 1/2 teaspoons poppy seeds

1 teaspoon Dijon mustard

8 cups torn fresh spinach

Makes 8 servings

To peel and section oranges, cut peel and white pith off with a sharp knife. Cut beside membranes to remove orange sections. Do this over a bowl to catch the juice, reserving 2 tablespoons for dressing. Combine orange sections with strawberries and onion in a large bowl.

In a small bowl, whisk together dressing ingredients. Add to fruit; toss gently to coat. Chill. Serve fruit salad on bed of fresh spinach, drizzling any dressing from the bottom of the bowl over top of salads.

Sesame Rolls

5 to 6 cups all-purpose flour

3 tablespoons sugar

5 teaspoons active dry yeast

1½ teaspoons salt

1 cup water

2/3 cup sour cream

½ cup butter, sliced

2 eggs, beaten

Egg wash: 1 egg beaten with 1 tablespoon water

Sesame seeds

Makes 24 rolls

In large bowl, combine 4 cups flour, the sugar, yeast, and salt. In small saucepan, combine water, sour cream, and butter. Heat over medium-low heat just until butter melts (110° to 120°F), stirring frequently. Add to flour mixture with two beaten eggs. Beat with wooden spoon until well combined. Stir in enough of remaining flour to make a soft dough that pulls away from sides of bowl. Turn dough onto floured surface. Knead dough until smooth and elastic, about 8 minutes.

Divide dough into 24 equal pieces. Roll each piece into a ball. Place balls on greased baking sheets. Cover with a cotton cloth or plastic wrap. Let rolls rise in warm place for about 1 hour, or until doubled in size.

Heat oven to 400°F. Snip five ½" deep cuts around top edge of each roll. Brush rolls with egg wash and sprinkle with sesame seeds. Bake one pan at a time for 15 to 18 minutes, or until rolls are golden. Remove rolls to wire rack to cool.

A Cup of Friendship

Sharing a proper cup of tea with friends is a relaxing and elegant activity. Choose a black tea, such as Earl Grey, English Breakfast, or Irish Breakfast tea. Loose-leaf teas are better than tea bags for brewing a pot.

To make a pot of tea, bring a kettle of water to a rolling boil. Swirl a little hot water in a teapot to warm it, then discard the water. Add tea leaves to pot (one heaping teaspoon per cup plus one extra for the pot). Pour boiling water over the leaves, stir, and cover. Let tea steep for 5 to 7 minutes. To serve, pour the tea through a small fine-mesh strainer. (Alternately, you may place tea leaves in a tea ball before adding to the pot. The tea just won't brew as strongly since the water can't flow around the leaves.)

Serve tea with milk, lemon slices, sugar, and honey.

Mystic Petits Fours

Cake:

- 1 pkg. (18.25 oz.) plain white cake mix (no pudding)
- 1 pkg. (3 oz.) raspberry-flavored gelatin
- 1/2 cup granulated sugar
- 1/4 cup all-purpose flour
- 1 cup vegetable oil
- 4 eggs
- 2/3 cup red raspberry purée*
- 1/2 cup milk
- 1/2 cup seedless red raspberry jam

Icing:

- 8 cups powdered sugar
- 1/2 cup water
- 1/2 cup light corn syrup
- 2 teaspoons vanilla or almond extract

Makes 24 petits fours

Heat oven to 350°F. Spray a jelly roll pan with nonstick spray. Line the pan with parchment paper. Spray again and dust with flour, shaking excess flour out of pan. Set pan aside.

Combine cake mix, gelatin, sugar, and flour in a large mixing bowl. Add remaining cake ingredients, except jam. Blend on low speed of electric mixer until combined. Scrape down sides of bowl. Beat at medium speed for 2 minutes. Pour into prepared pan. Bake on middle rack of oven for 25 to 30 minutes, or until cake springs back when lightly touched in center and it starts to pull away from sides of pan.

Cool in pan for 10 minutes. Run knife around pan edges to loosen cake. Turn onto cooling rack and remove paper. Place a second cooling rack over cake and invert it so it is right side up again. Cool completely.

Trim off edges of cake to make a 10½" × 14" cake. Shave the top off with a serrated knife to level it. Cut cake in half crosswise to make left and right halves. Spread jam over top of one cake half. Top with second half. Cut cake into twenty-four 1¾" squares. Place squares on wire rack set over a jelly roll pan to catch dripping icing.

For icing, combine all icing ingredients in the top of a double boiler. Whisk over simmering water until smooth and temperature reaches 110°F. Remove from heat, but keep pan over warm water so icing does not set up. Spoon warm icing over petits fours, coating tops and sides. To coat sides, use a palette knife or butter knife to spread icing over sides as it drips. The icing sets up quickly, so work fast to avoid a clumpy look. Icing caught in pan may be reheated and used again.

To make raspberry purée, thaw 2 cups frozen red raspberries, then press them through a sieve.

Decorating the Petits Fours with Drop Flowers

Decorator Icing:
6¼ cups powdered sugar
¾ cup vegetable shortening
½ cup milk
¾ teaspoon white vanilla
extract or almond extract

In a mixing bowl, beat sugar and shortening together at low speed of electric mixer. Beat in milk and vanilla until smooth. Divide icing in half, tinting half with green food coloring for leaves and the other half pink (or desired color) for the flowers. Practice making leaves and flowers on a plate before decorating petits fours.

1 Fit a pastry bag with a leaf tip. Fill bag with green frosting and twist end to close it. To make leaves, hold tip at an angle to the surface near the center of the petit four. Squeeze bag and hold the tip in place to let the frosting fan out to form the leaf base. Decrease the pressure, slowly pull the tip away, and lift slightly to draw the leaf to a point. Make two leaves on each petit four.

2 Fit a pastry bag with a drop flower tip. Fill bag with pink frosting and twist end to close it. To make flowers, hold bag perpendicular (straight up) with the tip touching the surface of the petit four. Squeeze bag, keeping the tip in the frosting until the flower is formed. Stop squeezing and pull tip away. For swirled flowers, twist the tip slightly while squeezing.

Note: *Tinted icing is available in tubes in the cake aisle of the supermarket. Decorator tips are sold with them and are screwed on the end. These are easy to use with virtually no clean-up.*

leaf tip

drop flower tip

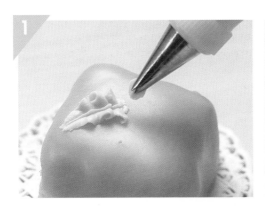

CUSTOMS

In the Middle Ages, a close female relative or friend of the bride was asked to swear that the bride was not being forced into marriage by her father. Thus began the traditional Maid of Honor, a role filled today by the bride's sister or closest friend. Among her duties, she signs the marriage license.

You're a Valuable
Part of Our
Wedding
Puzzle

rehearsal dinner

the relaxed atmosphere and casual serving style of a fondue dinner is perfect for this wedding eve gathering. Tasteful and entertaining, it is a pleasant diversion from the frenzied pace of last-minute detailing and a welcome contrast to the formality of the fast-approaching wedding. The groom's family traditionally hosts this dinner for the attendants and their significant others, giving the bride and groom and their parents a chance to acknowledge and pay tribute to all the special people who are helping to turn their wedding day dream into reality.

Playful bright colors set against a white background create a cheerful tone for this party.

Round tables, about 48" (122 cm) in diameter, conveniently seat six people around each fondue pot. Foods for fonduing are artfully arranged on small platters between place settings. Remove furniture from a large room in your home to accommodate this dining arrangement. Borrow or rent an assortment of fondue pots, one for each table suitable for cooking meats and vegetables, and at least two pots suitable for desserts. If you must purchase the pots, consider giving them as gifts to the attendants. ◆

You're a Valuable
Part of Our
Wedding
Puzzle

Fondue
Rehearsal
Dinner

September 10
right after
the rehearsal

at the home of:
Jane & Gary Phillips
732 Glenridge Pass
Edina

Please bring your puzzle piece
with you to the party.

Integral members of the wedding entourage feel recognized and appreciated by this unique invitation. The puzzle piece is both symbolic of the guest's importance and a clue to the pleasure-packed evening in store. ◆

MATERIALS

- Pieces from bride and groom puzzles (page 98)
- Text-weight paper in primary and secondary colors
- Glue stick
- Card-weight paper scraps of various colors
- Pearl cotton in the six primary and secondary colors
- Envelopes, 4¹/₂" × 5³/₄" (11.5 × 14.5 cm)

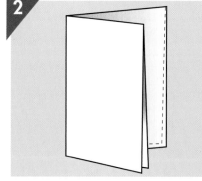

1 Create puzzles as on page 98. Test-fold a plain piece of paper, following step 2, below. Plan out and print the invitation message so part of it will be hidden under the front pocket-cover.

2 Fold paper in half from top to bottom. Then fold in half again from side to side, with open corners at lower right.

3 Open paper. Draw faint pencil line ¹/₁₆" (1.5 mm) to left of center vertical fold. Fold lower left quadrant diagonally, aligning horizontal fold to pencil line; crease diagonal fold. Repeat for upper left quadrant. Refold invitation, aligning diagonal folds. (Red lines are mountain folds; purple lines are valley folds.)

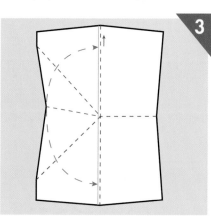

4 Glue single layers of front together along lower edge, forming pocket. Trace puzzle piece on different color card-weight paper; cut out. Glue to pocket front.

5 Cut 20" (51 cm) lengths of six pearl cotton colors; knot together at one end. Separate into groups of three; knot ends. Secure one end to a stationary surface. Twist from other end until cords are wound tightly and evenly on both sides of center knot.

6 Holding center knot, allow sides to twist around each other, forming six-color twisted cord. Knot ends together; trim off previous end knots.

7 Loop cord around puzzle piece; insert in card pocket.

Echoing the color-coded concept used to identify fondue forks, ribbon spokes in the six primary and secondary colors radiate from the fondue pot at the hub of each table. Cut wide grosgrain ribbon long enough to extend from the table center to a drop length of about 12" (30.5 cm). Secure ribbon to the white tablecloth, using double-stick tape or a strip of fusible web. ◆

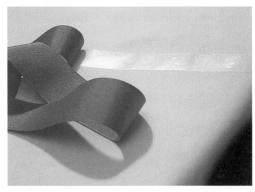

Water glasses are painted with polka dots in colors to match the individual place settings. Follow the manufacturer's directions for using glass paints. ◆

MATERIALS

- *Clear glasses with straight, smooth sides*
- *1" (2.5 cm) masking tape*
- *Sponge pouncers in two sizes*
- *Glass paints in red, orange, yellow, green, blue, and purple*
- *Paper plate*

1 Mask off the upper edge of the glass to about 1" (2.5 cm) below rim. Pour a small pool of paint onto a paper plate. Dip large sponge pouncer into paint; dab off excess. Pounce paint dot onto outer surface of glass. Repeat randomly around glass.

2 Paint small dots in open areas. Allow paint to dry thoroughly. Remove tape. Follow the paint manufacturer's directions for curing.

Cheerful jellybeans, in the six table colors, fill cellophane bags at each place setting. Each is tied with narrow grosgrain ribbon in the place setting color. Hanging place cards mark each guest's spot. ◆

Ramekins filled with dipping sauces are arranged around the base of the fondue pot. Some pots may have a rotating tray attached for holding the sauces. Otherwise individual sauces can be passed around the table. Fondue plates have separate divisions for holding the sauces and a larger space in the center for holding the cooked meats and vegetables. ◆

Cotton napkins in colors that match the ribbons are crisply starched and folded to form pockets for holding warm dinner rolls. ◆

MATERIALS

- Cotton fabrics in colors to match ribbons
- Sewing machine; thread

1 Make napkins 18″ to 20″ (46 to 51 cm) square, following the instructions on pages 142 and 143. Starch and press. Fold in half, with open edges at the top; press.

2 Fold lower corners up to meet at center top.

3 Flip napkin over so open edges are now at the bottom. Fold lower corners up to meet at center top.

4 Flip napkin over. Just before seating, tuck a warm dinner roll under the folds on the front of the napkin and place in the center of the plate.

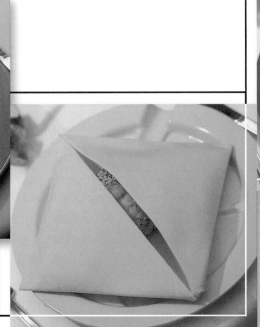

2

fold corners up to this point

3

HINT
Sew, starch, fold and stack napkins weeks before the wedding when you have more time.

Meats and vegetables for fonduing are artfully arranged on small platters. Meats, cut into thin strips are separated with fresh lettuce or herb sprigs. Guests share a platter of meats on one side and vegetables on the other, so passing is not necessary. ◆

Self-service coffee bar is set up with various flavors of gourmet coffee. Each carafe sports a simple ribbon tie and label. Overlapping napkins, turned on point, cover the bar and carry on the party color theme. ◆

Splashes of color dart from the flower arrangement on the coffee table. This low-profile arrangement (page 146) allows for easy conversation as guests assemble puzzles and enjoy the informal dessert and coffee. ◆

HINT

Select background music that complements the party theme. Keep it loud enough to be heard but soft enough for normal conversation.

Brightly colored flowers in a tall symmetrical arrangement grace the dessert buffet table. Flowers of different sizes and textures, as well as colors, combine effectively to make stunning arrangements. Follow the directions and tips for fresh flower arranging on pages 144 to 147. ◆

Puzzle

Puzzle pieces scattered over end tables and trays connect with the pieces each guest received in their invitation to complete pictures of the bride and groom. Guests can team up to complete their puzzles while waiting their turn for the dessert fondue. Make the puzzles yourself, using a computer, scanner, and printer. Or take photographs to a print shop that offers this service. Prepare several puzzles depicting the bride and groom at different stages in their courtship. ◆

MATERIALS

- *Color photos of the bride and groom*
- *Heat transfer puzzle kits that include heat transfer paper and precut 8" × 10" (20.5 × 25.5 cm) puzzle*
- *Computer; scanner; inkjet or laser printer*
- *Iron*
- *Colored dot stickers*

1 Scan the photo; enlarge to fit the puzzle format. Print the image on heat transfer paper.

2 Transfer the image to the puzzle surface, following the manufacturer's directions.

3 Place colored dot stickers on the backs of the puzzle pieces to identify which puzzle they belong to. Separate puzzle pieces.

Schedule

1 week or more ahead:
- Collect enough fondue pots, plates, and forks.
- Prepare homemade broth, if making it, and freeze.
- Make grocery lists.

3 days ahead:
- Get all groceries, except fresh vegetables, meats, and seafood.

2 days ahead:
- Make the following sauces: Horseradish Sauce, Citrus Barbecue Sauce, Mustard-Dill Dip, Hot Honey-Maple Mustard, and Ginger Soy Sauce.

1 day ahead:
- Make Chili Peanut Sauce.
- Get vegetables and meats (try to wait until the day of party to purchase seafood).
- Chop chocolate for dessert fondues.
- Strain raspberries for white chocolate fondue.

Morning of:
- Purchase and clean seafood.
- Partially freeze and slice meats.
- Arrange meats, chicken, and seafood on platters; cover and chill.
- Prepare vegetables. Arrange on serving platters; cover and chill.
- Combine broth ingredients in stockpots. Chill until 1 hour before serving time.
- Prepare and arrange dippers for dessert fondues on serving platters; cover and chill.
- Prepare tossed green salad, but don't add dressing yet.

1 hour before:
- Heat broths to a simmer.
- Measure dessert fondue ingredients; set aside.

½ hour before:
- Set out covered vegetable platters.
- Set out sauces.
- Fill fondue pots with broth and keep warm.
- Add dressing to green salad and toss.

Just before serving:
- Warm dinner rolls; tuck into napkins at each place setting.
- Set out meat platters.
- Prepare dessert fondues just before serving.

Fondue

Fondue is a great way to get people talking and laughing. The pace of eating is relaxed, allowing plenty of time to chat and get to know the future in-laws. There are a few basic types of fondue—the classic cheese fondues, oil fondues, broth fondues (hot pots), and of course, dessert fondues. This party features two broth fondues and two dessert fondues. They are easy to make, the mess is minimal, and they don't require special equipment or lots of attention.

How It Works

Broth is prepared on the stove and brought to the table, where it is kept hot over a flame. Platters of meats and vegetables are prepared for cooking, with special attention given to making them look attractive. Each guest spears a piece of meat or vegetable and places it in the broth to cook. Several sauces are served in ramekins and passed around the table to be spooned onto plates for dipping. Special fondue plates have divided sections to accommodate these sauces. After the food is cooked, it is transferred to the plate to enjoy with the sauces. Meanwhile, another piece of food is speared and put into the broth to cook.

Regular flatware is provided for eating the food. It is improper to eat from the long forks and they are very hot. Breads and a crisp tossed green salad are all that is needed to complete the meal.

Practical Matters

- Plan on no more than six people per pot of fondue. It's difficult to fit more than six fondue forks in a pot; they would cool the broth too much and slow the cooking.

- There are several types of fondue pots available: metal, electric, enameled cast iron, ceramic, or earthenware. Heavy ones that diffuse heat are best for dessert fondues since they minimize scorching. Metal pots work best for broth, since they'll keep it hot for cooking meats.

- Place pots on a heatproof, stable surface to protect tables and prevent tipping. Flat tiles or trivets work well.

- Arrange raw meats and seafood on separate platters from vegetables. Arrange vegetables as artfully as possible and separate raw meats with fresh lettuce leaves or herb sprigs.

- The broth becomes really flavorful after cooking all those meats and vegetables. When the fonduing is done, ladle the hot broth into cups with cooked pasta (like orzo) or rice to finish the meal.

The Recipes

The recipes on pages 102 to 105 are enough for one pot of fondue with dips to serve six people. All recipes are easily multiplied, and it's probably best to make a large stockpot full of broth if you plan to fill several fondue pots. The dessert fondues on page 107 shouldn't be more than doubled, however, for best results.

Basic Seasoned Broth

4 cups chicken broth
  (canned or homemade)

2 cups beef broth
  (canned or homemade)

2 cloves garlic, crushed

1 sprig fresh thyme

1 sprig fresh parsley

1 bay leaf

1 teaspoon whole peppercorns

Makes enough for 1 fondue pot

Combine all ingredients in saucepan. Bring to a simmer. Simmer for 15 minutes. Strain. Transfer to fondue pot.

Horseradish Sauce

1 cup sour cream

1/2 cup mayonnaise

2 tablespoons Dijon mustard

2 tablespoons prepared horseradish

1/2 teaspoon freshly ground pepper

Makes 1 1/2 cups

Combine all ingredients. Cover and chill up to two days ahead.

Citrus Barbecue Sauce

1 cup chili sauce

2 tablespoons brown sugar

2 tablespoons Worcestershire sauce

2 tablespoons lemon juice

1/2 teaspoon grated orange peel

Makes 1 1/4 cups

Combine all ingredients. Cover and chill up to two days ahead.

Mustard–Dill Dip

1 cup mayonnaise

2 tablespoons prepared yellow mustard

1/2 teaspoon dried dillweed (or 1 tablespoon snipped fresh dillweed)

1/2 teaspoon salt

1/2 teaspoon freshly ground pepper

1/8 teaspoon garlic powder

Makes 1 1/4 cups

Combine all ingredients. Cover and chill up to two days ahead.

Asian Broth

4 cups low-sodium chicken broth
(canned or homemade)

2 cups beef broth (canned or
homemade)

1/4 cup soy sauce

1/4 cup sliced fresh gingerroot

4 green onions, sliced

2 cloves garlic, crushed

1 teaspoon whole peppercorns

Makes enough for 1 fondue pot

Combine all ingredients in saucepan.
Bring to a simmer. Simmer for 15
minutes. Strain. Transfer to fondue pot.

Chili Peanut Sauce

1/2 cup hoisin sauce

1/2 cup crunchy peanut butter

1/2 cup chicken broth

3 tablespoons soy sauce

3 tablespoons honey

1 tablespoon chili paste with garlic

Makes 1 3/4 cups

Combine all ingredients in a
saucepan. Bring to a boil, whisking
until smooth. Remove from heat.
Cool. Cover and chill up to a
day ahead.

Hot Honey–
Maple Mustard

1/2 cup hot Chinese mustard

1/4 cup honey

1/4 cup pure maple syrup

Makes 1 cup

Combine all ingredients. Cover and chill up to two days ahead.

Ginger Soy Sauce

1/2 cup soy sauce (Japanese soy sauce, if available)

1/2 cup dry sherry

1/2 cup rice vinegar

1/4 cup finely chopped ginger

1/4 cup packed brown sugar

1 clove garlic, minced

1/4 teaspoon crushed red pepper flakes (optional)

Makes 1 1/2 cups

Combine all ingredients. Cover and chill up to two days ahead.

Meats and Seafood

Tender and lean cuts of meat, such as pork and beef tenderloin and chicken breast, are best for fondue. The meat will cook quickest if it is very thinly sliced. Partially freeze meat for easy slicing, then cut it about 1/8" thick. Shrimp, firm bay scallops, and lean white fish are the best seafood selections for fondue. In general, plan on 6 to 8 ounces of untrimmed meat and seafood per person.

Let beef and pork warm up at room temperature for up to 1 hour before serving. If it is straight from the refrigerator, it will be so cold that the broth will cool down and slow cooking. Don't warm up chicken or seafood.

Vegetables

Vegetables are great for fonduing and add a lot of flavor to the broth. Some can be cooked directly in the broth like the meat, but others should be boiled or steamed until tender-crisp. Good choices for raw vegetables are: shiitake or white mushrooms, red bell peppers, zucchini or yellow summer squash, and green onions. Partially cook vegetables like broccoli and cauliflower florets, carrot chunks, red potato chunks, and asparagus pieces. Cut all vegetables into bite-size pieces.

Dessert Fondues

Chocolate fondue is delicate and scorches easily. A heavy ceramic or an electric fondue pot works best, as the heat is not so intense. Don't use metal fondue pots. If this isn't possible, use a votive candle rather than a fuel source to keep the chocolate warm.

Dessert fondue dippers can include cubed pound cake or angel food cake, whole strawberries, sliced bananas, biscotti, gingersnaps, pineapple chunks, or dried fruit.

The Original Toblerone® Fondue

2/3 cup heavy whipping cream

4 bars (3 1/2 oz. each) Toblerone chocolate, finely chopped

1 tablespoon cognac or brandy

Makes enough for 1 fondue pot

In a heavy medium saucepan, bring the cream to a simmer over medium heat. Do not boil. Remove from heat and stir in Toblerone. Let stand for 3 minutes, or until Toblerone softens. Add cognac and whisk until smooth. Transfer to a heavy fondue pot. Serve immediately with desired dippers.

White Chocolate–Raspberry Fondue

1 1/2 cups frozen red raspberries

1 cup heavy whipping cream

1 lb. white chocolate, finely chopped

2 to 3 teaspoons cognac or rum (optional)

Makes enough for 1 fondue pot

Heat raspberries over medium heat until juicy, stirring occasionally. Press through a fine-mesh sieve and reserve juice.

In a heavy medium saucepan, bring the cream to a simmer over medium heat. Do not boil. Remove from heat and stir in chocolate. Let stand for 3 minutes, or until chocolate softens. Add cognac; whisk until smooth. Transfer to a heavy fondue pot. Swirl in raspberry juice. Serve immediately with desired dippers.

Note: *White chocolate is quite sweet; serve with less-sweet dippers, like biscotti or dried fruit.*

luau reception

Polynesian paradise, re-created in a tented yard, is the setting for a delayed wedding reception. Dressed in surfside casual attire, the newlyweds and their guests celebrate in the glow of torches, surrounded by romantic island music and the fresh scent of tropical flowers. Traditional Hawaiian dishes, tailored to feed a crowd with ease, are served from buffet tables laden with island bounty. ◆

Moonlight

and starshine, assisted by
candlelight, torches, and tiny
twinkle lights, illuminate the luau
tent. Tropical plants and island
paraphernalia add to the
ambiance in a somewhat tongue-
in-cheek way. Tent poles are
disguised as palm trees, buffet
tables wear flowing grass skirts,
and steam sputters from the top
of a "volcano" made from fruit
and tropical flowers. ◆

Colorful paper leis swing between pop-up palm trees in the luau invitations. This miniature island paradise surprise beckons your guests to a fun-filled celebration. Though the invitation may look complicated, it requires only a few simple steps. You can produce a large number of them faster by completing each step of the instructions for the total number needed before moving on to the next step. ◆

MATERIALS

- Sand-colored paper 8½" × 11" (21.8 × 28 cm) for pop-up insert
- Scissors; ruler
- Blank single-fold cards, 6¾" × 5" (17 × 12.5 cm) with envelopes
- Glue stick
- Flower-shaped punch
- Vellum or plain paper in three tropical colors
- Two palm tree cutouts per invitation or green card-weight paper to make cutouts
- Fine cotton or jute cord
- Crewel needle

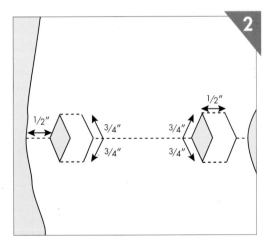

1 Print reception invitation message on sand-colored paper; two copy boxes spaced equally, turned in landscape direction. Cut apart. Round corners and sides in slightly irregular shape.

2 Fold insert in half. Cut two ¾" (2 cm) slits ½" (1.3 cm) apart, ½" (1.3 cm) from each side. Open insert. Indent (page 139) a line connecting each set of slits at the top and bottom; fold on indented lines to form pop-up supports. Glue insert to inside of card, keeping pop-up supports free.

3 Punch out flowers, keeping them in piles according to color. Cut out palm trees, if necessary. Thread needle with a 45" (115 cm) length of cord. Insert needle through back of palm tree, then through nine flowers of alternating colors, then through front of other tree. Repeat four times, for a total of five sets. Prepare additional lengths of cord until you have the number of sets needed.

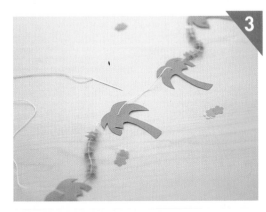

4 Cut cord in 8" (20.5 cm) lengths, keeping complete sets of trees and flowers on each length. Knot ends.

5 Glue trees to pop-up supports. Allow to dry completely before closing cards.

A handcrafted guest book and pen feature tropical flowers, bamboo, and seashells. The luau host presents each guest with a lei upon arrival and encourages them to write a short aloha message to the newlyweds. ◆

HINT
If your street is crowded, have your guests park in a nearby public parking lot and arrange shuttle service.

Palm trees flanking the luau entrance cleverly disguise the tent poles. Made from vent hose and fabric with spiky silk leaf tops, the trees simply slide on the poles before erecting the tent. ◆

MATERIALS

- *3" or 4" (7.5 or 10 cm) diameter semirigid expandable vent hose, 8-foot (2.44 m) length per tree*
- *Lightweight cotton fabric for trunk*
- *Sewing machine; thread*
- *Spiky silk leaf cluster*
- *Duct tape*

1 Cut fabric strips 1½" (3.8 cm) wider than hose circumference with length equal to twice the desired height of the trunk. Fold in half lengthwise, right sides together. Stitch ½" (1.3 cm) seam. Turn right side out.

2 Slide fabric sleeve onto unextended vent hose trunk. Slide trunk onto tent pole before setting up tent. Stretch vent hose to desired height, distributing fabric fullness evenly up and down "tree trunk."

3 Insert leaf cluster into trunk top. Secure leaves to pole with duct tape.

This lazy net hammock cradles a treasure-trove of gifts for the newlyweds. Twinkling lights are woven through the net holes around the outside of the hammock. ◆

HINT
Spread a bamboo mat on the grass for heavier gifts or to catch the overflow.

Crisp white dinner napkins, folded into lotus shapes, float on ocean-blue tablecloths at each guest's place. ◆

A sandy beach surrounds flickering candles in the center of each table. Glass cylinders are encircled with tropical reeds or thin bamboo shoots. Small seashells strewn along the shore add to the tropical fantasy. One medium-size conch shell at each table anchors a speared list of guests who will be seated there. ◆

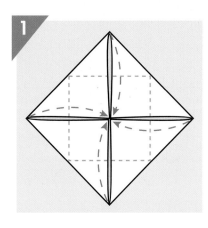

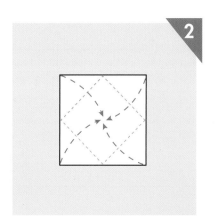

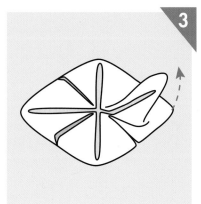

1 Fold all four corners to the center; repeat twice.

2 Turn folded napkin over and fold all four corners to the center.

3 Hold center points with one hand. With other hand, pull four folded corners out from under napkin and up to form petals. Repeat at sides and again at corners, forming 12 petals.

MATERIALS

- *Reeds or thin bamboo shoots*
- *Three glass cylinders in graduated sizes; candles*
- *Rubber bands*
- *Raffia*
- *Candles*
- *Fine white sand*
- *Small seashells*
- *Medium-size conch shell*
- *Potting soil*
- *Fine-textured green plant, such as baby's tears or fern*
- *Ecru parchment paper*
- *Bamboo skewer*

ELAINE DEWALT

LINDA MONROE

BILL MONROE

STEPH JOHNSON

ARLENE THOMAS

JIM THOMAS

LAURIE POWERS

TOM POWERS

1 Cut reeds in various lengths, slightly taller than cylinder sides. Stand them around cylinder; secure with rubber bands. Tie raffia over rubber bands. Repeat for each cylinder. Insert candles.

2 Stand candles in table center. Mound white sand around candle bases. Scatter small seashells in sand.

3 Plant small amount of greenery in conch shell. Print out guest list for table on parchment paper. Spear list with bamboo skewer, and insert into plant.

HINT
Select long-burning pillar candles that stand low enough in the cylinders to be out of the breeze.

Breezy grass skirts dress the buffet tables. Separate buffet stations for main course foods, punch, and wedding cake facilitate the traffic flow for a large crowd. ◆

F̲ragrant and beautiful flower leis (necklaces) and hakus (head wreaths), worn by the bride and groom, distinguish them as the guests of honor. Fresh orchid leis can be purchased from specialty florists or from various web sites. ◆

A bountiful mound of fresh fruits and tropical flowers forms a natural volcano in the center of the buffet table. A gurgling fountain spouts from the top as "steam" settles down over the "mountainside." In reality, the steam is a fine mist created by a small electronic device placed in a shallow bowl of water. The mist maker can be ordered from a fountain parts supplier (see source list on page 159). ◆

MATERIALS

- 18″ to 20″ (46 to 51 cm) round tray, 12″ (30.5 cm) round tray, 8″ (20.5 cm) clay pot, 6″ (15 cm) clay pot

- Floral adhesive clay; vinyl tape

- Clear glass or plastic bowl, 6″ to 8″ (15 to 20.5 cm) diameter, about 6″ (15 cm) deep

- Mist maker

- Fresh whole fruits in sizes ranging from pineapples to grapes: 3 to 4 pineapples, 6 to 8 pears, 6 to 8 papayas, 12 bananas, 8 star fruit, several clusters of small grapes (substitute waterproof plastic fruit as desired)

- Fresh or waterproof artificial tropical blossoms

- Water

- Electrical supply; extension cord

1 Invert large pot in center of large tray; secure with floral adhesive clay. Repeat for small pot and small tray; secure to bottom of large pot. Secure bowl to bottom of small pot. Place mist maker in center of bowl; tape cord to outside of bowl.

2 Slice pineapples in half. Place them facedown on bottom tray, with leaves pointing to one side. Arrange bananas on top tray, curving in opposite direction. Layer remaining fruit, one variety at a time, graduating in size to the top of the bowl. Finish with clusters of grapes attached to the sides of the bowl, trailing down over the "mountainside." Insert blossoms randomly.

3 Fill bowl with water. Connect mist maker to electrical source, following manufacturer's directions. Add water partway through the evening, if level gets too low.

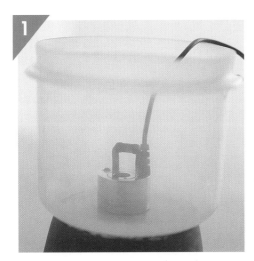

Wedding trip

photos and memorabilia are cleverly displayed in a fantasy sand dune. Photos are inserted into slits at the ends of bamboo stakes standing firmly in a rustic, sand-filled bucket and propped in coconut shells. ◆

MATERIALS

- *Wedding photos; access to color copier or scanner and color printer*
- *Tag board*
- *Photo-mount adhesive*
- *Mat knife; cutting surface*
- *Hollow bamboo stakes*
- *Electric mini lights, rubber band, duct tape*
- *Rustic wooden bucket*
- *White sand*
- *Drill and drill bit slightly larger than bamboo stakes*
- *Whole coconuts*
- *Wedding trip memorabilia*

1 Photocopy wedding photos. Adhere to tag board. Cut out photos as desired. Cut slits in ends of bamboo stakes; insert mounted photos.

2 Cluster mini lights; wrap wires with rubber band. Tape to inside front of bucket; hang plug end over back rim. Fill bucket with sand, hiding wires.

3 Drill holes in coconuts, pour out liquid. Insert photo stakes into sand and coconuts. Connect light wire to electrical source. Mound sand on display surface; arrange display items.

Refreshing tropical punch is a welcome thirst quencher after a spin on the dance floor. An ice ring garnished with lime slices and cherries adds a colorful touch while it cools the punch. Keeping the punch bowl filled and chilled is an easier task when you freeze several ice rings ahead of time and serve a prepared punch. ◆

MATERIALS

- 2 cups crushed ice
- 2½ cups pineapple tidbits, drained
- Ring mold with 6½-cup capacity
- 15 maraschino cherries with stems
- 7 lime slices
- Prepared punch

1 Combine ice and pineapple. Spoon ice mixture into ring mold. Arrange cherries and lime slices over ice mixture. Pour punch over fruit to fill. Freeze.

2 Dip mold into warm water for 10 to 15 seconds. Carefully unmold ice ring; store in plastic bag in freezer. Place ice ring fruit-side up in punch bowl.

Schedule

1 week or more ahead:

- Make grocery lists.
- Make cake layers for coconut-lime cake and freeze.

3 days ahead:

- Get fruit that needs to ripen.

2 days ahead:

- Get remaining groceries.

1 day ahead:

- Make pineapple upside-down cake; chill.
- Assemble and frost coconut-lime cake; chill.
- Toast coconut for sweet potatoes.
- Make Lomi Lomi Salmon.
- Prepare or purchase macaroni salad, if desired.

Morning of:

- Cut up pork and peppers for kabobs.
- Prepare ingredients for Chicken Long Rice.
- Prepare fruit kabobs, cover with plastic and chill.
- Prepare tossed green salad, if desired, but don't add dressing.

2 hours before:

- Peel and roast potatoes; set aside.

1½ hours before:

- Soak skewers for pork kabobs and place pork in marinade.
- Prepare Chicken Long Rice.

1 hour before:

- Assemble pork kabobs; start grilling after they are assembled.
- Prepare long-grain white rice, if desired.

½ hour before:

- Glaze potatoes.
- Add dressing to green salad and toss.
- Set out fruit, breads, and salads.

Just before serving:

- Set out all food.
- Cut cakes just before serving.

Kalua Pork Kabobs

20 thick wooden skewers

6 lbs. boneless pork loin roast, cut into 2" cubes

2 cups water

1½ teaspoons liquid smoke

⅓ cup kosher salt

6 red, green, or yellow bell peppers, cut into 2" chunks

Makes 20 servings

Soak skewers in water for 30 minutes. In large bowl, combine pork, water, and liquid smoke. Let stand for 30 minutes, stirring occasionally. Prepare grill for medium direct heat. Drain pork and sprinkle with salt. Thread pork cubes on skewers with bell pepper chunks. Grill for 15 to 20 minutes, or until pork is just slightly pink in the center. Serve kabobs on skewers, or remove pork and peppers from skewers to a large serving platter.

Notes: *Cooking time will vary depending on how crowded the grill is. There should be about 1" of space between kabobs. If you don't have enough grills to cook all the kabobs at once, grill them in batches and keep cooked kabobs hot on a baking sheet in a warm oven, covered with foil.*

This recipe is easily doubled.

Chicken Long Rice

1½ oz. dried shiitake mushrooms

1 bundle (3.85 oz.) long rice
(bean threads)*

4 lbs. boneless skinless chicken breasts

¼ cup vegetable oil

4 cloves garlic, minced

3 quarts chicken broth

½ cup soy sauce

½ cup slivered gingerroot

½ cup thinly sliced green onions

Makes 20 servings

Place mushrooms in a bowl. Cover with boiling water. Let stand for 30 minutes. Drain. Cut mushrooms into strips. Set aside. Prepare bean threads as directed on package. Drain. Cut into 2" lengths. Set aside.

Cut chicken into 1" cubes. Heat oil in large skillet over medium heat. Add chicken and garlic. Sauté for 6 to 8 minutes, or until browned. (For best results, sauté chicken in batches.) In a stockpot, combine chicken, mushrooms, long rice, broth, soy sauce, and gingerroot. Bring to a boil over medium-high heat. Reduce heat to medium-low. Simmer for 20 to 30 minutes, or until chicken is tender. Ladle into serving dish and sprinkle with green onions.

Long rice (bean threads) are long white noodles that turn clear when cooked. You can find them in the Asian section of your supermarket.

Note: *This recipe is easily doubled.*

Coconut Sweet Potatoes

12 orange-colored sweet potatoes
  (7 to 8 lbs.)

1/4 cup olive oil

Salt and pepper to taste

1 cup butter

2 cups brown sugar

1 cup water

1/2 cup grated coconut, toasted*

Makes 20 servings

Heat oven to 425°F. Peel sweet potatoes and cut into 1" chunks. Toss with oil, salt, and pepper. Spread potatoes on baking sheets. Roast for 20 to 25 minutes, or until browned and tender, turning chunks over once. Set aside.

In large pan, melt butter over medium heat. Add sugar and water. Simmer for 5 minutes. Reduce heat to medium-low. Add sweet potatoes, stirring to coat. Cook for 5 to 7 minutes, or until potatoes are glazed and heated through. Spoon potatoes into serving platter and garnish with toasted coconut.

*To toast coconut, spread it on a baking sheet. Bake at 325°F for 6 to 8 minutes, stirring often.

Note: When doubling this recipe, roast potatoes in batches. For glaze, increase butter to 1 1/2 cups, sugar to 3 cups, and water to 1 1/2 cups.

Lomi Lomi Salmon

24 oz. smoked salmon, shredded

8 medium tomatoes, seeded and finely chopped (5 cups)

2 cups thinly sliced green onions

1 cup finely chopped sweet yellow onion

1/2 cup ice water

Salt to taste

Makes 10 cups

Combine all ingredients in a large bowl. Mix well. Chill for several hours or overnight.

Kauai Kabobs

Kiwis, peeled and sliced

Pineapple, peeled and sliced

Grapes

Star fruit, sliced

Strawberries

Wooden skewers

Prepare fruit. Thread desired fruit pieces on skewers in attractive pattern. Arrange on serving plate. Cover with plastic and chill until serving time.

Pineapple Upside-Down Cake

20 slices canned unsweetened
  pineapple (2 cans [20 oz. each])

1/2 cup butter, melted

1 1/2 cups packed brown sugar

20 maraschino cherries

Batter:

2 1/3 cups all-purpose flour

1 1/2 teaspoons baking powder

1/2 teaspoon baking soda

1/2 teaspoon salt

1 1/2 cups sugar

3/4 cup butter, softened

4 eggs

1 teaspoon vanilla extract

1 cup buttermilk

Makes 20 servings

Grill pineapple slices over medium direct heat for 3 minutes per side. Set aside. Pour melted butter in 10" × 15" sheet pan to coat bottom. Sprinkle brown sugar evenly over butter. Arrange pineapple slices in pan and place a cherry in the center of each ring. Set aside.

Heat oven to 350°F. In a medium mixing bowl, combine flour, baking powder, baking soda, and salt. In a large mixing bowl, cream sugar and butter together at medium speed of electric mixer. Add eggs and vanilla. Beat until combined, scraping sides of bowl as necessary. Alternately beat in buttermilk and flour mixture at low speed of electric mixer until combined.

Spread batter over fruit in prepared pan. Bake for 25 to 30 minutes, or until wooden pick inserted in the center comes out clean. Run knife around edge of pan to loosen sides of cake. Immediately turn cake out onto large serving platter. Let cool.

Note: *Cake is best on the day it is made, but it may be covered with plastic wrap and refrigerated up to a day ahead.*

Make 2 or 3 cakes for reception.

Coconut-Lime Wedding Cake

Cake:

1 pkg. (18.25 oz.) white
  cake mix with pudding

1¼ cups water

⅓ cup vegetable oil

3 eggs

Filling:

¼ cup fresh lime juice

3½ tablespoons butter

2 tablespoons water

1 teaspoon grated lime peel

⅓ cup sugar

4½ teaspoons cornstarch

Pinch salt

1 whole egg

1 egg yolk

Frosting:

8 oz. cream cheese, softened

3 tablespoons milk

1 teaspoon coconut flavoring

6 to 7 cups powdered sugar

2 cups grated coconut, fluffed

Makes 16 servings

For cake, heat oven to 350°F. Grease and flour three 8" round cake pans. Set aside. Place cake mix, water, oil, and eggs in large mixing bowl. Blend on low speed of electric mixer for 1 minute. Increase speed of mixer to medium and beat 2 minutes more, scraping sides of bowl as necessary.

Divide batter evenly among prepared pans. Bake for 20 to 25 minutes, or until cakes pull away from sides of pans and spring back when lightly pressed with your finger. Place pans on wire rack to cool for 10 minutes. Run a knife around edges of pan to loosen cakes and invert cakes on cooling rack. Cool completely. Wrap cakes in plastic and freeze for at least 1 hour.

For filling, combine lime juice, butter, water, and lime peel in medium saucepan. Heat over medium heat until butter melts. Remove from heat. In medium mixing bowl, whisk together sugar, cornstarch, and salt. Whisk in egg and yolk. Gradually whisk in hot juice mixture. Return mixture to pan. Cook over medium heat for 5 to 7 minutes, or until filling is thick and bubbly, whisking constantly. Remove from heat. Place filling in bowl and cover with plastic wrap touching the surface of the filling. Chill completely.

For frosting, beat cream cheese in large mixing bowl at high speed of electric mixer until very creamy. Add milk and coconut flavoring. Beat at low speed to combine. Beat in powdered sugar 2 cups at a time, beating well after each addition. Frosting should be stiff but spreadable.

To assemble the cake, brush crumbs off frozen cake layers and level off any rounded tops with serrated knife. Place first layer on serving platter. (Protect platter from mess by placing pieces of wax paper or parchment paper around cake, tucking it just under the cake. Pull pieces away when frosting is complete.)

Spread about ½ cup frosting on top of first layer, building it up slightly around edges to make a "dam" to hold in filling. Spread ⅓ cup lime filling inside the frosting dam. Top with second layer and repeat with frosting and filling. Top with third layer. Freeze cake for 1 hour.

Rebeat the frosting. Spread frosting over top and sides of cake. Immediately, sprinkle remaining coconut over top and press into sides of cake before frosting has a chance to set up. Store cake in refrigerator until ready to serve. Serve chilled or at room temperature.

Note: *Frosting tends to set up as it sits. Just rebeat with electric mixer as necessary while frosting the cake.*

TRADITIONS

It is customary for the bride and groom to cut and eat the first piece of wedding cake together. Once upon a time, superstition suggested a bride would be childless if she did not cut the first piece. Today this charming ritual by the bride and groom simply signifies the sharing of their love.

entertaining
help

where to begin

Some of us are born list makers, going so far as to write down reminders to make lists. Others of us boast the ability to "keep it all in our heads." When it comes to planning and hosting a wedding party, task schedules and shopping lists are the keys to success, no matter how large or small the guest list. Checking off items on a to-do list can be rewarding in itself, but pulling off a successful party without a single hitch is an accomplishment to brag about. With careful organization, the process of orchestrating the perfect party is as entertaining as the party itself. The Party Planning Timetable, opposite, is a good place to start. Along with the recipes for every party, you will find a schedule for preparing the food, which can be incorporated into your general timetable. You may have additional tasks to include, relative to the size and theme of the party you are hosting.

Aside from shopping lists, keep a detailed log of the invited guests, their addresses, and telephone numbers. The bride and groom will probably have to furnish you with most of this information. Take careful notes about who has responded and any other pertinent information—a guest will be arriving late, must leave early, or is allergic to seafood.

Budget is another big consideration. Make a list of all the expenses you anticipate and try to estimate the total cost. From this point you can cut back in the areas that are least important to you or spend a little more where your wallet allows. There is always the option of asking someone to cohost the party with you, splitting the costs. Cohosting or even hosting by committee has other advantages: sharing ideas, sharing tasks, and sharing the limelight.

party planning timetable

4 to 8 Weeks Ahead:
- Inform the honored guest(s) of your desire to host the party; select the date and time.
- Determine the guest list with the assistance of the honored guest(s).

3 to 4 Weeks Ahead:
- Plan the party theme, decorations, and menu.
- Make and send invitations.
- Test recipes and craft items you are unsure of.
- Decide what you will wear.
- Make arrangements for rental items, such as a tent, tables and chairs, or dinnerware.

2 Weeks Ahead:
- Make separate shopping lists for groceries and bar items.
- Make lists and shop for decorations and craft materials (other than fresh flowers).
- Make any handcrafted items, such as favors, place cards, or table linens.
- Call to schedule any helpers.

1 Week Ahead:
- Finalize the guest list, calling guests who have failed to respond.
- Buy groceries for menu items that will be made ahead and frozen, nonperishable groceries, and bar items.
- Prepare and freeze/store any menu items that can be made in advance.
- Select and inspect all tableware and serving pieces.
- Plan the seating arrangement or buffet table layout.
- Order fresh flowers.
- Order fresh bakery items, if serving a large crowd.
- Check in with the rental company.

2 Days Ahead:
- Clean out the refrigerator.
- Buy any fresh fruit that needs to ripen.
- Pick up flowers and other fresh plant material needed for decorations.
- Select music.

1 Day Ahead:
- Make centerpieces, corsages, or other fresh floral accents.
- Clean and decorate the house.
- Press table linens; fold napkins.
- Set the dining table or set out serving pieces on the buffet table.
- Thaw frozen menu items.
- Buy any fresh baked goods.
- Make room in the coat closet.

Party Day:
- Prepare the food following time schedules provided.
- Set up the bar; chill beverages as necessary.
- Run and empty the dishwasher.
- Empty garbage cans.
- Stock bathrooms with guest towels, soap, and extra toilet paper.

hosting alfresco

Entertaining outdoors requires careful planning to avoid a few pitfalls. The most obvious, of course, is the possibility of inclement weather. If the number of guests invited to the party can easily fit inside your home, you need only move the party indoors. However, for larger parties, it may be necessary to establish Plan B, either selecting an alternate date or an alternate location.

If you wish to reserve an alternate date, be sure to indicate this possibility on the invitation. On the day of the party, if the weather is questionable, you must call all of the guests to let them know whether or not the party is postponed. Unfortunately, by the time you make this decision, you will have already prepared much of the food. Selecting an alternate location, such as a nearby pavilion or hall, can be costly, since you may have to pay a rental fee, even if you don't end up using the facility.

Renting a tent gives you the freedom to have your party, rain or shine. If the party is given during the day, a tent provides shade as well as shelter from an occasional shower. At night, a tent ceiling also provides a surface from which light can be reflected to illuminate the scene.

Given the number of guests, the planned activities, and a site location inspection, the tent rental company can provide you with different options and suggestions for the size and style of tent you need.

Here are a few other important details to consider when renting a tent:

- Make sure the tent rental company carries liability insurance. The tent materials should be flame-retardant.

- Inquire about community ordinances and any permits that may be required before putting up the tent.

- Consider adding a full or partial floor if dancing is on the agenda.

- Consider how you will handle restroom facilities—whether you want your guests to trudge back and forth into your house or use portable rental facilities that will add to your expenses.

- Make sure your home's electrical supply can bear the extra load required for outdoor lighting, music, and any miscellaneous electrical needs.

Bugs can be a real annoyance at an evening party, especially if food is served after dark. The lights that illuminate the party scene are a beacon for those unwelcome pests. Citronella candles and lamps may ward off mosquitoes but should be kept around the perimeter of the party where they won't interfere with the aroma and taste of the food you've worked so hard to prepare. Consider having the lawn and garden area sprayed for bugs earlier in the day to minimize the problem. As a last resort, you could offer repellent to your guests. For daytime entertaining, keep the food covered with lids, napkins, or mesh tents to keep flies and bees away.

Serving food outdoors requires a little extra planning and precaution. Decide how you will transport food from your kitchen to the buffet, for instance. Setting up the buffet tables close to the back door minimizes the number of steps you or your helpers have to take. Arrange ways to keep foods at their proper serving temperatures. If you don't have enough refrigerator space, make arrangements with a close neighbor or rent several ice chests.

Here are a few more pointers for serving food outdoors:

- Keep perishable foods refrigerated until just before serving or grilling. For example, keep trays of pork kabobs (page 124) cold and ready for grilling at a luau reception by storing them in a large cooler near each grill. Likewise, dish up cold foods in medium-size containers and keep them on ice under the buffet table to be quickly swapped with empties.

- Clear empty plates away immediately after the meal, and keep garbage cans covered and out of sight away from the party area.

- Plan a specific time for serving the meal and clearing the tables rather than offering an all-day or all-night buffet.

making invitations

Handmade invitations, tailored to the party theme, are the first indication to your guests and honorees of your enthusiasm and panache as a host. Impressive cards can be produced with some very basic skills and minimal time, especially when lettering and internal messages are generated on a computer.

papers

Specialty paper stores carry paper for card crafting in a variety of weights, finishes, and sizes, in a complete rainbow of colors. Your invitations can be created from blank ready-made cards with matching envelopes or cut from text-weight, card-weight, or cover-weight paper, depending on the fold method. Consider the materials lists given for each invitation in this book to be suggestions to get you started. Ultimately your selection of papers, envelopes, and embellishments depends on what is available to you.

Machine-made papers have a grain, meaning the fibers lie in the same general direction. This is evident when paper is folded, rolled, torn, or cut; the paper is more flexible and "cooperative" along the grain. Whenever possible, card-weight and cover-weight paper should be folded with the grain. Handmade papers do not have a grain, because the fibers lie in all directions.

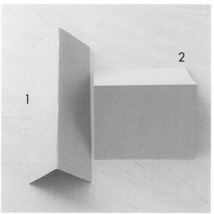

Card-weight paper that has been creased across the grain (1) produces a rough, uneven fold. The same paper folded with the grain (2) produces a clean, smooth fold.

Cover-weight paper (1) is firm and rigid, suitable for single-fold cards and card covers. It should be scored or indented (page 139) before folding. Card-weight paper (2), slightly less rigid and lighter in weight than cover-weight paper, is suitable for single-fold cards and pop-up cards. It should be indented before folding. Text-weight paper (3) is thinner and less rigid, so it can be folded multiple times without scoring or indenting. Vellum (4) is a translucent paper used for overlays, envelopes, and inserts when a see-through effect is desired. It is available in many weights, in white or colors, printed or plain. Heavy handmade papers (5) offer textural interest and strength for special effects.

tools & techniques

Most of the techniques used for making invitations involve cutting or creasing the paper. There are a few tools and and special techniques that give your invitations a professional look.

Paper can be cut with scissors, but accuracy and straight lines are better achieved with the use of a ruler, mat knife, and self-healing cutting surface. A specialty paper trimmer, which combines all three tools in one, squares, measures, and cuts paper with ease. Decorative-blade scissors, in many different cutting patterns, cut paper with fancy edges. Paper punches in a wide range of shapes and sizes cut decorative or functional holes, leaving cutouts that are useful for embellishments. Specialty corner slot punches cut decorative corners with slits for holding photos or name cards.

Text-weight paper can usually be creased successfully in both directions. Card-weight and cover-weight paper, however, should be indented or scored before creasing, to ensure a smooth folded edge.

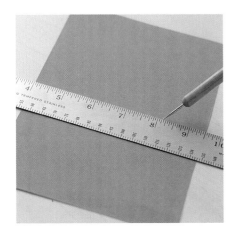

Indenting: Lightly mark the intended fold line on the inside of the fold. Align a metal ruler to the line. Indent the line, sliding a fine-point stylus or a dull butter knife along the ruler edge. Fold the paper with the indented line on the inside.

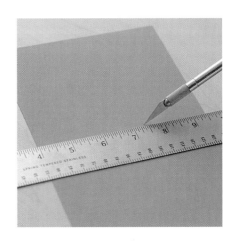

Scoring: Lightly mark the intended fold line on the outside of the fold. Align a metal ruler to the line. Holding a mat knife with the blade facing upward, score the line, sliding the knife tip along the ruler edge and cutting gently through only the upper layer of fibers. Fold the paper with the scored line on the outside.

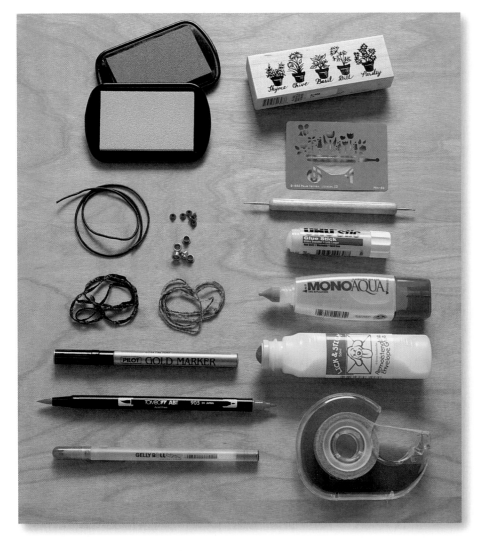

There are many other tools and supplies useful for decorating and personalizing your invitations. Rubber stamps and ink pads decorate invitations with detailed artwork. Subtle, elegant raised designs are created with brass embossing plates and a stylus. Paper-backed double-stick tape, glue sticks, and liquid glues with fine-point tips give you several options for adhering papers and embellishments. Watercolor pens with both fine and broad tips add soft, precisely placed color. Gel pens and metallic pens give handwritten messages a special look. Grommets, laces, and decorative cording are just a few of the many other materials that can be used to create special effects.

invitation messages

Your invitation must include all the information that your guests need to know in order to fulfill their roles: why, when, where, and any special instructions, such as what type of gift to bring or how to dress. Most likely you'll appreciate an accurate count of the number of guests to expect, so also include a response request and your phone number.

Along with the start time, give the day of the week as well as the date of the party, to avoid confusion and help your guests fix the occasion in their minds. It is usually not necessary to give an ending time, unless you are hosting an open house.

Give complete information about where the party will be held. Don't assume that everyone remembers where you live and how to get there. If the event will be held somewhere other than your home, a detailed map with parking information is helpful.

Computer word-processing programs offer a variety of fonts from which to choose. Try to select fonts that have a style consistent with the theme and mood of your party. For instance, to convey the semiformal nature of an engagement party, select a font that looks sophisticated and classy:

Erica and Glen have decided to tie the knot! Let's celebrate with them.

For an event that requires casual dress and a laid-back attitude, use a font that looks fun:

LUAU ATTIRE ENCOURAGED!

Handwrite the invitation message for a truly personal touch, such as for the Bridesmaids' Tea Party. If you simply don't trust your handwriting to be legible, at least add a short personal note and sign your name at the bottom. Each of your guests will feel as though the event is planned especially for them.

If you intend to use your home computer for printing your invitations, become familiar with the options provided by your printer. Check that it will accept the paper size and weight you intend to use, and always run a sample test to be sure. For conserving paper, instructions may suggest that you plan two or more identical copy boxes, print out the messages, and cut them apart. Trial runs will help you determine if you have spaced the copy boxes accurately.

envelopes

Ideally envelopes are ¼" (6 mm) larger than the invitation. Some common paper sizes for single-fold invitations and their corresponding envelope sizes are listed in the chart at right.

If the invitation you create does not fit into one of these standard size envelopes, you can make matching envelopes in the correct size. Take note, however, of the smallest size envelope the U.S. mail service will accept, and also be aware that square envelopes require extra postage.

ENVELOPE SIZE	PAPER SIZE (to be folded in half)
3⅝" × 5⅛" (9.3 × 13 cm) (smallest accepted for U.S. mail)	5" × 7" (12.5 × 18 cm)
4⅜" × 5¾" (11.2 × 14.5 cm)	5½" × 8½" (14 × 21.8 cm)
4¾" × 6½" (12 × 16.3 cm)	6¼" × 9¼" (15.7 × 23.6 cm)
5¼" × 7¼" (13.2 × 18.7 cm)	7" × 10" (18 × 25.5 cm)

MATERIALS
- Ruler
- Scissors
- Text-weight paper
- Paper-backed double-stick tape
- Remoistenable envelope glue

1 Draw a rectangle ¼" (6 mm) larger than the finished size of the invitation. Draw ¾" (2 cm) flap extensions on the sides; round the flap corners.

2 Draw equal rectangles, about ⅔ the height of the envelope, extending from the top and bottom. Mark points ¼" (6 mm) in from the outer corners of these flaps; redraw the sides to angle in from these points.

3 Fold in the short side flaps. Fold the lower flap up; apply narrow double-stick tape to the outer edges of the lower flap and adhere to the side flaps.

4 Apply remoistenable envelope glue to the upper edge of the upper flap; allow to dry. Insert the invitation; fold the upper flap down. Remoisten and seal the envelope.

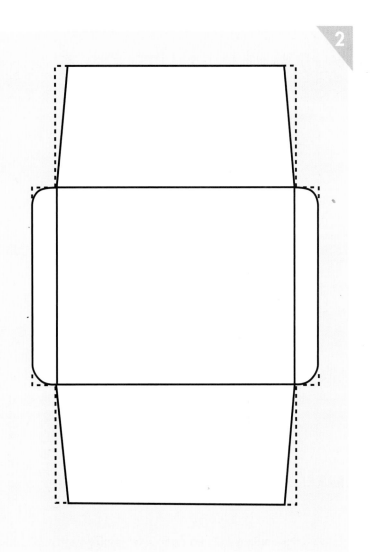

making napkins

Paper napkins are perfectly suitable for informal gatherings but occasions seem more special when you use cloth napkins. Purchasing cloth dinner napkins for a party of fifteen people can take a big chunk out of your party budget. However, you can make the napkins more affordably with fabric of your choice and one free evening.

Dinner napkins range in size from 16″ to 20″ (40.5 to 51 cm); cocktail napkins are about 12″ (30.5 cm). Look for fabric that measures at least 48″ (122 cm) across so you can cut three dinner napkins or four cocktail napkins from one width of fabric. Napkins must be made perfectly square for successful folding.

Though cloth napkins are often reversible, printed fabrics are also suitable. Natural fiber fabric, such as cotton or linen, is absorbent, easily laundered, and will hold creases for special napkin folds better than synthetic fabric.

Fringe Method

Loosely woven fabrics and fabrics with woven-in checks and plaids are especially suited to this method.

1 Mark fabric at desired size plus 1″ (2.5 cm). Pull lengthwise and crosswise yarns to ensure straight, even fringe; cut along the space left by the missing yarn.

2 Stitch narrow zigzag ½″ (1.3 cm) from edge, pivoting ½″ (1.3 cm) from corners. Pull out yarns to fringe each edge.

Serger Method

If you have a serger, you can make many napkins quickly, following this method.

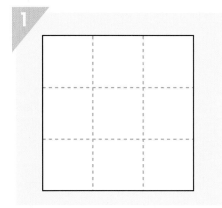

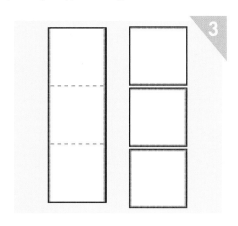

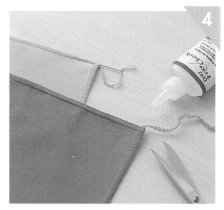

1 Mark napkin dimensions on the fabric, following the grainlines. Use pencil or chalk on tightly woven fabric; pull out yarns on loosely woven fabric. Leave a small margin on the fabric ends.

2 Set the serger for a balanced 3-thread overlock, 4 to 5 mm wide and 1 mm long. Thread both loopers with texturized nylon thread; use regular thread in the needle. Test and adjust.

3 Serge on marked lines across the fabric, cutting it into strips; serge the unfinished edges. Then serge each strip into square napkins, leaving tail chains at corners. Serge the unfinished edges of each napkin.

4 Thread tail chains onto a darning needle and draw back under the stitches at the corners. Or apply a drop of fray preventer at each corner, allow to dry, and snip off thread tails.

Conventional Sewing Method

A neat, narrow, double-fold hem is suitable for any tightly woven lightweight to mediumweight fabric. To reduce sewing time, complete each step for the total number of napkins before moving on to the next step.

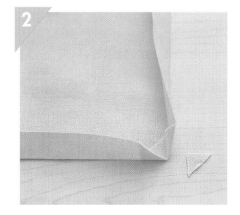

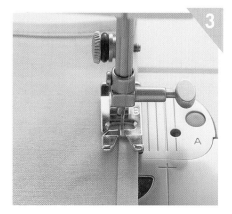

1 Cut napkins 1" (2.5 cm) larger than the desired finished size, following the grainlines.

2 Press under 1/4" (6 mm) double-fold hem on each side. Unfold the corner; fold diagonally so the inner pressed folds align. Press the diagonal fold; trim corner as shown. Repeat at each corner.

3 Refold, mitering corners. Edgestitch inner fold to secure hem. Edgestitch again near outer edge, if desired.

fresh flower arrangements

Fresh flowers add a luxurious touch to wedding showers, engagement parties, and receptions. Using year-round and seasonal varieties from your own garden or purchased from the florist, you can create beautiful arrangements to decorate the dining room table, coffee table, entry area, or buffet.

A centerpiece on the dining room table should be short so it does not interfere with conversation. Because it is seen from all sides, it is usually symmetrical. A buffet arrangement can be taller for more impact. It, too, should be symmetrical if the buffet is in the center of the room. If the buffet table is against a wall, the arrangement can be three-sided.

The long-lasting flowers listed at right are excellent choices because they can be arranged ahead of time. If the arrangement will be made in advance, select compact blossoms that will open to full beauty by the day of your party.

A fresh arrangement can be displayed in any container that holds water. For baskets, terra-cotta pots, or decorative metal pots, use a plastic waterproof container as a liner.

Follow these basic guidelines for working with fresh flowers:

• Cut rose stems diagonally under water, at least 2" (5 cm) from the end, using a sharp knife. When stems are not cut under water, air bubbles form at the ends, preventing water from rising up the stem.

• Cut stems for most fresh flowers diagonally, using a sharp knife, to increase water absorption. Snap the stems of chrysanthemums.

• Remove any leaves that will be covered by water or floral foam; leaves left in the water will shorten the life of the flowers.

• Remove stamens from lilies to prevent pollen from falling on and discoloring petals and table linens.

• Crush the stems of woody plants and evergreens with a hammer to increase water absorption.

• Add cut-flower food to the water and add fresh water daily. Keep arrangements out of direct sunlight. With the exception of orchids and succulents, mist the blossoms in the arrangement to keep them fresh longer.

Long–Lasting Fresh Flowers

VARIETY	AVAILABLE COLORS	LASTS
Allium	Purple and white	10 to 12 days
Alstroemeria	Many colors	8 to 10 days
Aster	Pink, purple and white	8 to 10 days
Baby's breath	White	7 to 14 days
Carnation	Many colors	7 to 14 days
Chrysanthemum	Many colors	10 to 12 days
Cornflower	Blue, pink, purple, and white	8 to 10 days
Forsythia	Yellow	12 to 14 days
Freesia	Yellow, pink, purple, and white	5 to 7 days
Fruit-tree blossom	Many colors	10 to 14 days
Gingerroot heliconia	Red and pink	8 to 10 days
Heather	Purple and mauve	10 to 14 days
Leptosporum	White and reddish pink	5 to 7 days
Liatrix	Purple and white	7 to 10 days
Lily	Many colors	7 to 10 days
Orchids	Many colors	5 to 10 days
Ornithogalum	White, yellow, and pink	10 to 14 days
Rose	Many colors	5 to 7 days
Star-of-Bethlehem	White	10 to 14 days
Statice	Many colors	14 to 21 days
Sunflower	Yellow with brown	14 to 21 days
Yarrow	White and yellow	10 to 14 days

making a fresh floral centerpiece

1 Soak floral foam in water containing flower food for thirty minutes. Cut foam, using knife, so it fits container and extends 1" (2.5 cm) above the rim. Secure with floral tape.

2 Cut greenery sprigs 5" to 8" (12.5 to 20.5 cm); trim away any leaves near ends. Insert sprigs into foam, with longer sprigs around outside and shorter sprigs near center.

MATERIALS

- Floral foam for fresh flowers
- Flower food
- Sharp knife
- Waterproof container
- Floral tape
- Two or more varieties of greenery
- Flowers in three sizes

3 Insert largest flowers into foam, placing one stem in center and several stems on each side to establish height and width of arrangement. Space remaining large flowers evenly.

4 Insert smaller flowers into arrangement, one variety at a time, spacing evenly, so arrangement appears balanced from all sides.

making a tall arrangement

MATERIALS

- Vase
- Clear waterproof floral tape
- Two or more varieties of greenery
- Tall, linear floral material, such as devil's claw heliconia, curly willow, or branches
- Flowers in three sizes

1 Make a grid over the mouth of the vase, using clear waterproof floral tape.

2 Insert first variety of greenery into vase, placing taller stems in center near back and shorter stems at sides and front. Add remaining varieties of greenery.

3 Insert tall linear materials, spacing them evenly.

4 Insert largest flowers, one variety at a time, spacing them evenly throughout to keep arrangement balanced on three sides.

5 Insert second largest flowers into arrangement, spacing evenly. Insert smallest flowers into arrangement to fill any bare areas.

seating plans

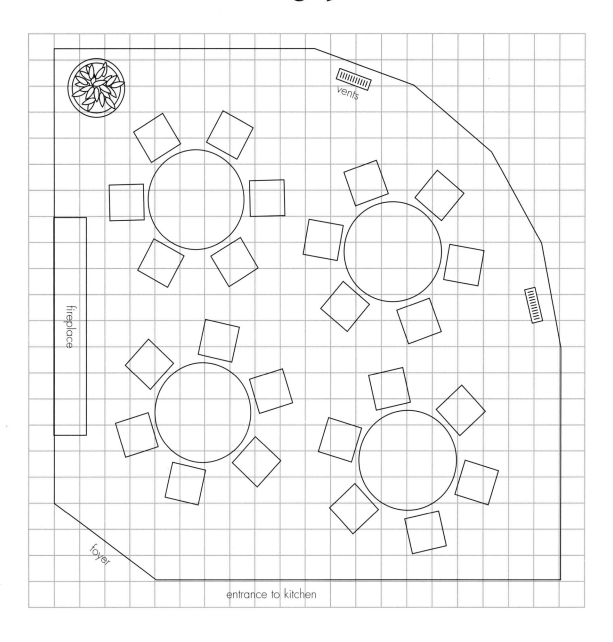

Entertaining in your home may pose some challenges when it comes to seating all of your guests or establishing an efficient buffet arrangement. Analyze the space in each room and draw out a seating plan on graph paper to make the most efficient use of the space you have. Draw the room to scale, noting doorways, fireplaces, and any other obstacles. Include the location of any suspended light fixtures. Consider moving furniture out of a large family room or living room to set up multiple tables for a large group. Perhaps store the furniture in the basement or garage.

Rental companies have round and rectangular tables in

many sizes, usually with inexpensive plywood tops that must be covered with tablecloths. Of course, the table linens can be rented as well. As a general rule, round tables offer the most efficient seating. The chart below shows common sizes of tables, the number of people each will comfortably seat, and the tablecloth size required. This is based on the estimate that each place setting uses a space 24″ (61 cm) wide and 18″ (46 cm) deep. Allow 18″ (46 cm) for chair depth and another 24″ (61 cm) moving space behind chairs. With this in mind, round tables, set up to mesh like cog wheels, can often comfortably seat more people than rectangular tables in the same space.

TABLE SIZE round	SEATS	TABLECLOTH short	TABLECLOTH floor length
36″ (91.5 cm)	4 or 5	60″ (152.5 cm)	94″ (239 cm)
48″ (122 cm)	6 to 8	70″ (178 cm)	108″ (275 cm)
60″ (152.5 cm)	8 to 10	84″ (213.5 cm)	120″ (305 cm)
72″ (183 cm)	10 to 12	90″ (229 cm)	132″ (335 cm)

TABLE SIZE rectangular	SEATS	TABLECLOTH short	TABLECLOTH floor length
36″ (91.5 cm) square	4	52″ (132 cm) square	
30″ × 48″ (76 × 122 cm)	4 to 6	52″ × 70″ (132 × 178 cm)	
30″ × 60″ (76 × 152.5 cm)	6	60″ × 84″ (152.5 × 213.5 cm)	For floor-length cloths
36″ × 60″ (91.5 × 152.5 cm)	6 to 8	60″ × 84″ (152.5 × 213.5 cm)	on rectangular tables,
30″ × 72″ (76 × 183 cm)	6 to 8	60″ × 84″ (152.5 × 213.5 cm)	secure skirting to
40″ × 72 (102 × 183 cm)	8	60″ × 84″ (152.5 × 213.5 cm)	short tablecloths.
30″ × 96″ (76 × 244 cm)	8 to 10	60″ × 120″ (152.5 × 305 cm)	
40″ × 96″ (102 × 244 cm)	12	60″ × 120″ (152.5 × 305 cm)	
48″ × 108″ (122 × 275 cm)	12 to 14	60″ × 120″ (152.5 × 305 cm)	

setting the table

The universal "rules" for the arrangement of plates, flatware, and glassware at each place setting are designed for convenience and efficiency, at least for right-handed people. Because the settings are followed consistently, left-handed people become accustomed to the placement and adapt their eating mannerisms. A change in the expected arrangement would cause confusion and reflect unfavorably on the entertaining savvy of the host. Creativity need not be stifled entirely, though. Napkins, for instance, can be folded in many intriguing ways and placed in various positions in the place setting.

Here are some of the basic table setting guidelines:

- Set out only the tableware items necessary for the menu, including a glass for each beverage you intend to serve.

- To free up some table space, set out some items, such as the dessert plate and fork and coffee cups and saucers, after the main plates are cleared.

- Arrange flatware in the order in which each piece will be used, progressing from the outside in toward the plate.

Glassware

Stemmed glassware designed for a specific purpose is distinguished by its shape. From left to right: oversized balloon glass for water; rounded glass for red wine; straight-sided glass for white wine; all-purpose wine glass; tall, slim champagne flute; snifter (for brandy or cognac); dessert wine glass.

The Informal Place Setting

In anticipation of a relaxed serving style and simple meal, an informal place setting includes these elements:

- The dinner plate is in the center of the setting, about 2" (5 cm) from the table edge or centered on a placemat.

- Flatware is arranged in order of use, from outside inward, with handle bottoms aligned to the plate edge. Forks are to the left of the plate; the salad fork on the far left indicates the meal will be started with a salad. The knife, with cutting edge inward, is placed to the right of the plate. If a spoon is needed for the meal, it is placed to the right of the knife.

- The napkin, with folded edge inward, rests to the left of the forks.

- A beverage glass is slightly above and to the left of the knife tip.

The Formal Place Setting

A formal setting indicates a more sophisticated serving style and a more complex meal. Follow the basic guidelines for the informal setting, with these additions:

- The soup spoon to the right of the knife indicates soup will be served.

- A bread plate is placed above the forks.

- Wine glasses in front of the water glass indicate that white wine will be served with the first course, followed by red wine.

- A dessert spoon and/or fork are placed above the plate, parallel to the table edge; the fork handle to the left, the spoon handle to the right.

Optional Place Settings

You may opt to set each place with a charger, setting the plate or bowl for each course on the charger as the meal progresses. Alternatively, salad or soup may be served before seating, with the plate or bowl set in the center of the dinner plate or charger.

serving the food

After preparing a fabulous meal for your guests, you'll want the serving style to be equally as impeccable and impressive. Allow about an hour at the beginning of the event for guests to arrive, mingle, and have a drink before starting the meal. This also gives you time to greet them all properly and do a little mingling yourself before hiding away in the kitchen to tend to last-minute details.

There are many ways to serve the food to your guests; the method you choose depends on the party mood (formal or casual), the number of guests, and the food itself.

Plating the food in the kitchen and serving each guest individually allows you to arrange the food in an eye-pleasing manner and control portions. After seating, wine is poured, reaching from each guest's right side. Then filled plates are served from the guests' left side. If a salad or soup is already in place when guests are seated, wait until everyone is finished and then remove the plates or bowls and salad forks or soup spoons, reaching from the guests' right. After clearing away all plates and utensils used for the main course, repeat the procedure with dessert and coffee.

Family-style service is a bit more relaxed. Platters and bowls of food are passed around the table, allowing each guest to

around the table, allowing each guest to decide on his own portion. The host begins passing, serving himself last. There is no set rule on the direction in which to pass the food; passing in both directions may speed up the process, especially for larger groups. The host clears the table after the main meal and brings dessert and a coffee carafe to the table to pass.

Buffet service is a great way to go when you lack table seating or are serving a large group. Self-service encourages guests to mingle and keeps the traffic flowing. Plates, napkins, and utensils are placed at the beginning of the buffet table if guests are free to find seating in another room. In this case, bringing beverages to them lessens their need to juggle. Or tables for seating can be set with napkins, utensils, and glasses, leaving only plates at the buffet. While buffet service frees the host to mingle with the guests and enjoy the party, someone does have to keep a watchful eye for platters that need replenishing. A wait staff may walk among the guests offering appetizers or desserts. This is especially suitable for finger foods that taste best piping hot from the oven. Likewise, the wait staff gathers used plates and utensils, so guests aren't left wondering where to put them. Consider enlisting the help of a few young adults in your neighborhood or friends from outside the honored guests' social circle.

Combining two or more serving styles throughout the evening often works best. For instance, you may offer appetizers via the wait staff, choose plated or family-style service for the main meal, and set up a dessert buffet in another room.

setting a buffet

Buffet service gives you an opportunity to showcase the foods you have prepared in an impressive, inviting manner. Careful selection of serving pieces, complementary garnishes, and strategic placement on the buffet ensure that each dish will receive rave reviews, even before tasting.

Select serving pieces that are consistent with the party theme. Matched pieces are not always possible or necessary. Use glass or chrome pieces to reflect evening candlelight at a semiformal affair like the engagement party. Get creative by using unexpected vessels for serving the food, such as garden trugs and clay pots for an outdoor garden shower.

Serve hot foods in smaller vessels that can be refilled easily and often. Always remove the vessel to the kitchen for refilling, returning it full, rather than refilling at the buffet. Or switch a full plate for a nearly empty one, if you have enough serving pieces. For large gatherings, use chafing dishes to keep hot foods hot, but avoid overcooking them.

Setting up separate buffets for appetizers, the main course, desserts, and beverages keeps traffic flowing smoothly and encourages people to mingle and help themselves. The dining room table and sideboard are obvious places to set up the buffets, though other surfaces should be considered as well. For instance, a living room coffee table works well for a dessert buffet. Sofa tables, side tables, kitchen counters, and portable tables give you more options.

Buffets can be set up with access to only one side or access to both sides. Plates and napkins are set at the beginning. For a full meal buffet, the food is arranged in order, starting with the main course, vegetables or salads, grains and potatoes, and breads. If flatware and glassware must be picked up at the buffet, they are placed at the end of the buffet line, so guests don't have to juggle them while serving themselves. To minimize congestion at the end of the line, a beverage station can be set up away from the main buffet table.

When serving a large number of guests, such as for the luau wedding reception, the food order can be reversed, ending with the main course. This ensures that, starting with an empty plate, guests do not take oversized portions of the more expensive main course foods. Also, the hot foods are at the end of the line, closer to the kitchen, for frequent refilling. A mirror-image buffet is set with plates picked up at the center and two lines moving in opposite directions down the buffet.

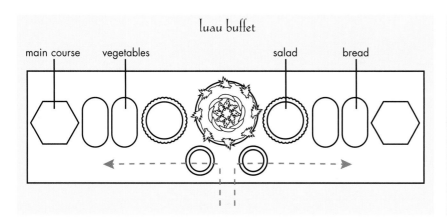

luau buffet

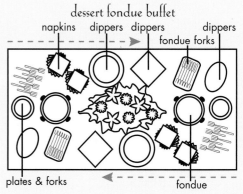

dessert fondue buffet

Here are a few more helpful tips and ideas for successful buffet service:

- Enlist servers to stand behind the main course foods in the buffet line at a large gathering. While speeding the process, you are also better able to control portion sizes.

- Provide a serving utensil for each item in the menu, including bread or rolls and any dessert that is not already plated. Also, provide a spoon rest for items that must remain covered, such as those in chafing dishes or Crock-Pots.

- Tie a cloth napkin on the lid handle of a hot chafing dish to protect your guests from burning their fingers.

- Place risers under the tablecloth for perching foods at various heights. These may be as simple as inverted cake pans or sturdy boxes.

- Label foods that are not easily recognizable, for the convenience of guests with food allergies or aversions.

- For seated buffets, invite guests, one table at a time, to the buffet line. This will encourage an orderly traffic flow, and you'll be sure everyone has had a turn.

- When guests are eating from their laps, provide plenty of surfaces for setting beverages, such as end tables, coffee tables, TV trays, or ottomans.

- Allow ample time for everyone to finish eating and return for seconds before clearing empty plates.

- Clear serving vessels and utensils from the main course buffet before opening the dessert and coffee buffets. A short "break in the action" allows the host preparation time and ensures that some guests will not be eating dessert before others have started the main course.

wine basics

You don't have to be a wine connoisseur to host a successful party. With some basic knowledge about the different kinds of wine and how to serve them, your wine-serving savvy will go unquestioned. If you are truly a novice, the vast range of wines available may leave you baffled, especially because wine names usually refer to the region where the grapes were grown or to a specific grape variety. But here's a quick primer to get you heading in the right direction.

Wines are broadly classified in the following categories:

- Still wines (with no effervescence) include red, white, and rosé (blush). In simple terms, red wines are made from red grapes, white wines from white grapes, and rosés are made from red grapes but have very little contact with the skins and stems, from which much of the color is derived. Wine is further classified according to its sweetness; nonsweet wines are referred to as dry, sec, or brut, with brut being the driest or least sweet.

- Sparkling wines, including champagnes and spumantes, are characterized by effervescence. They, also, are further categorized according to their sweetness.

- Fortified wine, such as sherry or port, has been enhanced with brandy or some other spirit.

- Aromatic wine, such as vermouth, has been enhanced with herbs or spices.

- Vintage wine is made with 95% of the grapes harvested in a specific year, which is printed on the label. Non-vintage wines are made from grapes harvested from several years, and a date is not noted on the label.

Wine bottles should be stored on their sides so that the corks do not dry out and shrink, which could allow air to enter the bottle. For optimum life, wines should be stored in a dark, still environment at about 55°F.

The temperature at which wine is served is the key to optimum taste and enjoyment.

- Full-bodied red wines, such as Merlot, are served at a slightly cool room temperature, about 65°F.
- Light-bodied red wines, such as Pinot Noir or red Burgundy are served cool, around 55°F.
- Chardonnay and other dry white wines are served slightly chilled.
- Sweet white wines and sparkling wines are served chilled, but not ice-cold.

Chill wine in the refrigerator for two hours before serving, and remove to let it stand for a half hour or less to warm to the right temperature. Chilling wine for a longer period of time can dull its aroma and flavor. Or place unopened bottles in a bucket of ice and water for up to 15 minutes before opening and serving. If you forget to chill the wine, place it in a freezer for a few minutes, but don't forget it there, because frozen wine is worthless. Whatever you do, don't toss an ice cube into it, or you'll blow your cover!

You'll find a variety of corkscrews and pullers on the market. Make sure you know how to use the one you select and test it out before the night of the party. If the cork breaks apart into the wine, which may happen if the cork is dried out or your technique is less than perfect, pour the wine into a decanter and let the cork pieces settle out before serving it.

Older wines and heavy red wines often have deposits in the bottle and should be decanted before serving to avoid pouring the deposits into the glass. Pour slowly, stopping when you reach the deposits. Red wines should be allowed to "breathe," softening the harsh tannin (astrigency) of the wine and releasing more flavor, before drinking. Decanting the wine also serves this purpose most efficiently. Just opening a bottle and letting it stand for a few minutes only exposes a tiny surface area inside the neck of the bottle to the air. If not decanted, pour red wine into a wide-mouthed wine glass and let it breathe before drinking.

Uncorking champagne requires a little finesse—you're not hosting a victory shower! Make sure the bottle has not been agitated or chilled to near freezing. The cork is already under a lot of pressure and either condition could cause it to explode. Remove the wire and foil, keeping the cork turned away from faces. Drape a cloth napkin over the end and grasp the cloth-covered cork with one hand while turning the bottle with the other. When you feel the cork pop out, remove the cloth and pour the champagne. The napkin will keep the cork under control and catch any foam.

The proper glasses for wines are shown on page 150. Red wine is served in a wide-mouthed glass with a deep bowl to allow it to breathe. This also gives wine lovers room to swirl the wine in the glass, releasing more flavor and aroma to the nose. White wine is typically served in a straight-sided, smaller glass, so it remains chilled while drinking. The tall, narrow shape of a champagne flute exposes a minimal surface to the air, preserving the beverage's effervescence and chill.

To make yourself look like a real expert, have on hand a small selection of wines at their proper temperatures, including a full-bodied red wine (Merlot or Cabernet Sauvignon), a dry white wine (Chablis or Chardonnay), and a slightly sweet rosé (white Zinfandel). Your guests will be impressed when they see you pouring into the proper size and shape glass. To really wow their socks off, tie a cloth napkin around the neck of the bottle to catch errant drips, which can be prevented by simply giving the bottle a slight twist as you finish pouring each glass. Enjoy!

Index

Sources

Craft Supply Stores
(ribbons, paints, silk flowers, containers,
general crafting supplies)

Fabric Stores
(fabrics, ribbons, notions, general sewing
supplies)

Florists
(fresh flowers and floral arranging
supplies, leis)

Paper Craft Stores
(paper and supplies for making
invitations, rubber stamps, embossing
templates)

Party Rental Centers
(tables, chairs, linens, tents)

Party Supply Stores
(paper products, decorations, novelties)

Fountain Builder
1841 CR 977
Ignacio, Colorado 81137
970-883-5346
www.fountainbuilder.com
(fountain pumps and accessories)

Hancock Fabric Stores
www.hancockfabrics.com
(fabrics, ribbons, silk flowers, general
crafting supplies)

Hobby Lobby Creative Centers
www.hobbylobby.com
(general crafting supplies)

Jo-Ann Fabric & Craft Stores
www.joann.com
(fabrics, ribbons, silk flowers, general
crafting supplies)

Michaels Arts & Crafts Stores
www.michaels.com
(general crafting supplies)

Paper Depot
www.paperdepot.com
(paper and supplies for making
invitations, rubber stamps, embossing
templates)

Sweet Celebrations
800-328-6722
www.sweetc.com
(baking and cake decorating supplies)